How to Make Money Trading Stocks & Shares

Summary

Stock is the primary investment in many individual investors' portfolios. It is a stake in a publicly-traded corporation on your country's stock exchange. Ordinary stocks and preferred stocks are the two main categories. People purchase and sell stocks based on their expectations of business earnings or profits. The Dow Jones Industrial Averages and the S&P 500 indexes monitor common equities.

Stock refers to the transfer of a member's fully paid-up shares into a single fund. While the denomination of stock varies, all shares have the same denomination. Being a shareholder is important because you are entitled to a percentage of the company's earnings. Retained earnings, on the other hand, continue to reflect the value of a stock. The stock market is a secondary capital market for buying and selling equity shares of publicly traded companies.

The number of shares held by a person in relation to the total number of outstanding shares determines ownership. Dividends and capital appreciation are the two main avenues for profiting from shares. If one invests in shares, they can expect to profit from capital appreciation or gains on their initial investment (principal). The earnings or gains from stock might be as high as 100% or more. While investments are hazardous, the expected return is favorable.

The majority of stock that people invest in is common stock. Preferred stock differs from ordinary stock in that preferred stockholders are guaranteed a higher payout upon the company's dissolution. Common stock is a component of a corporation's ownership, with stockholders entitled to a proportionate share of any leftover assets if the company is dissolved. With the correct investment strategy, it can be done securely and with minimal probability of long-term losses. Long-term stock market investment has shown to be a profitable method of creating wealth.

All stock analysis aims to determine if a security's market value is correct. A derivative is a contract that grants the buyer the right, but not the responsibility, to purchase or sell the underlying asset by a defined date (expiration date) One may choose between a call option and a put option. American options can be exercised at any moment before they expire; European options only on the expiration date. Day trading is the act of purchasing and selling securities on a single trading day. The vast majority of day traders are well-educated and financially secure.

Long-term investors must be professional and patient because they must be ready to accept some risk in exchange for higher profits in the long run. Using options as an effective hedge against a falling stock market is a common example. Options may be used to protect your assets against a downturn in the same way you would insure your home or car. Understanding the risk-reward relationship is an important part of developing your investment philosophy. Trading strategy is a very particular process for determining at which price points you will join and exit deals.

Expert analysts are more likely to employ this form of analysis than typical investors. Technical analysis is the study of a stock's current day performance in order to forecast its movement the next day and if you analyze it well, you get paid well.

Table of Content

How to Make Money Trading Stocks & Shares

Chapter 01: Basics of Stocks and Shares

Chapter 1.1: Understanding Stock

Stock is the primary investment in many individual investors' portfolios, and it is generally purchased and sold on stock exchanges (though private transactions are possible). These transactions must adhere to federal regulations meant to protect investors from misleading practices. Stock investments have historically outperformed most other investments throughout time, and most online stockbrokers sell these assets.

A stock usually referred to as equity, is a financial instrument that represents ownership of a corporation's share. Stockholders can have access to a portion of the corporation's assets and earnings based on the number of shares they possess. The stock units are known as "shares."

How can we distinguish between stock and shares? It is a stake in a publicly-traded corporation on your country's stock exchange. If you hold a share in a corporation, you have a claim on its future earnings.

There are two ways to profit in the stock market. The first is a gain in stock value. When you buy shares in a corporation, for example, if you buy 1000 McDonald's shares for $80 each, you can sell them for a higher price if the price rises after a certain period of time, such as if it climbs to $150 per share after a year. So you invested $80,000 and can now sell it for $150,000? The second approach is dividends. For example, if McDonald's declared a $2 per share dividend on December 1, 2022, and you acquired 1000 shares on or before that day, you will get $2,000.

How Stocks Work

Companies sell stocks to raise capital to expand their operations, launch new products, or pay off debt. The "initial public offering" is the first time a corporation sells stock to the general public (IPO). Stockholders can resell their shares on the stock market after the IPO, where prices are determined by supply and demand.

The more goods available for purchase, the lower the price. The more individuals that buy a stock, the greater the price. People generally purchase and sell stocks based on their expectations of business earnings or profits. If traders feel a company's earnings are high or will rise further, the stock price rises.

One approach for shareholders to earn a profit is to sell their shares at a higher price than where they were obtained. If a firm does poorly and its shares lose value, you may lose some or all of your investment when you sell.

Dividends, which are quarterly payments dispersed on a per-share basis from a company's earnings, are another method of shareholders' profit. It is a method of rewarding and incentivizing investors (the actual owners of the firm) to invest. It is especially important for companies that are profitable but not fast expanding.

The third and riskier approach to profit from equities is to use derivatives, which are based on underlying assets like stocks and bonds. Stock options provide you the right to purchase or sell a stock at a certain price by a specified date.

A call option is the right to purchase at a specified price. When the stock price rises, you profit by purchasing it at a cheaper price and selling it at a higher price. A put option is the right to sell something at a specific price. When the stock price falls, you profit. In such an instance, you buy it at the lower price of tomorrow and sell it at the agreed-upon higher price.

Chapter 1.2: Types of Stock Trading

Ordinary stocks, on the one hand, and preferred stocks, on the other, are the two main categories.

Common Stocks

The Dow Jones Industrial Averages and the S&P 500 indexes monitor common equities. When they are traded, their values change. Common stockholders have the right to vote on corporate matters such as the board of directors, mergers and acquisitions, and takeovers.

Common investors, on the other hand, are paid last, after bondholders and preferred shareholders, if a company declares bankruptcy and liquidates its assets.

Preferred Stocks

Preferred stocks are similarly ownership stakes in a firm, but they do not have voting rights. Because dividend payments are set, holders know the exact amount of return to expect on dividends. Preferred stocks can be transformed into a different type of ownership.

Other Types of Stocks

Beyond those fundamental divisions, there are additional ways to categorize stocks.

Stock Industry Sectors

Stocks can also be classified according to the characteristics of the business that issued them. These several groups cater to the various demands of stockholders. Stocks are classed by their industry sector, which includes:

- **Basic materials:** Natural resource extraction companies
- **Conglomerates:** Global companies in different industries
- **Consumer goods:** Retail suppliers are businesses that produce products for sale in stores.
- **Financial:** Banks, insurance, and real estate firms
- **Healthcare:** Healthcare providers, health insurance firms, medical equipment suppliers, and pharmaceutical businesses
- **Industrial Goods:** Manufacturing companies
- **Services:** Companies that deliver things to customers
- **Technology:** Computers and software
- **Utilities:** Electric, gas, and water companies

Growth Stocks

Stocks can also be classified according to their potential and value. Growth companies are projected to rise rapidly, but they rarely pay dividends. Companies may not even be profitable currently, but investors anticipate the stock price will climb. These are often newer enterprises with a lot of opportunities for expansion and new business models.

Value Stocks

Dividends are paid by value stocks since the stock's price is not projected to grow significantly. Because these are often huge, established enterprises, the market overlooks them. Savvy investors believe the prices are too low for what the firms provide.

Blue-Chip Stocks

Blue-chip stocks are properly valued and may not develop rapidly, but they have shown to be dependable corporations in solid industries throughout time. They provide dividends and are thought to be more secure investments than growth or value equities. They are also known as "income stocks."

Chapter 1.3: Understanding Share

Shares are fractional ownership interests in a corporation. Shares are a sort of financial instrument used by certain firms to facilitate the fair distribution of any declared surplus earnings in the form of dividends to their stockholders. A stock with no dividend payments does not disperse its income to its owners. Instead, they look forward to furthering stock price growth as business profits rise.

Owners of a firm have the option of issuing preferred shares or ordinary stock to investors. In exchange for funds required to expand and run the business, companies issue equity shares to investors.

Unlike debt capital, which is acquired through a loan or bond issue, equity has no legal obligation to be repaid to investors, and shares do not pay interest even if they are allowed to pay out dividends from their profits. From little partnerships or LLCs to large international organizations, almost all businesses issue shares of some type.

The founders or partners of privately held businesses or partnerships own the stock. Shares of small businesses are sold to outside investors on the primary market as they expand. Friends and relatives may be among them, followed by angel or venture capital (VC) investors. If the business keeps expanding, it might try to obtain more equity money by selling shares to the general public through an IPO (IPO). Once a company's stock is listed on a stock market following an initial public offering (IPO), the shares are said to be publicly traded.

Types of Shares

1. Preference shares

This sort of share grants some preferential rights over other share types, as the name implies. Preference shareholder's principal advantages are:

When it comes to receiving a dividend, or a portion of the company's profits, they are given first consideration.

Preference shareholders have priority in receiving payment in the event of company closure.

Preference shares also come in three sub-types:

- **Preference shares over time:** Before any dividend is paid to equity shareholders, cumulative stockholders have the right to receive arrears. For instance, if market downturns prevented the payment of the dividends on preference shares for the years 2017 and 2018, preferred shareholders would be entitled to collect dividends for all prior years in addition to the current one.
- **Shares of non-cumulative preference:** No dividend is payable to Non-Cumulative Shareholders. These investors only receive a dividend when the business is profitable. The previous year's dividends were not paid.
- **Equities with convertible preference:** These shares are convertible, as their name suggests. Shareholders who are convertible may change their preference shares into

equity shares at a later date. However, the company's Articles of Association (AoA) must approve the conversion of shares.

2. Equity shares

Ordinary shares are another name for equity shares. Equity shares make up the majority of the company's issued shares. The secondary or stock market sees active trading of this kind of share. These stockholders are eligible to vote at corporate meetings. Additionally, they have a right to receive any dividends declared by the board of directors. The dividend paid on these shares, however, is not a fixed amount and could change annually depending on the company's profitability. Dividends are paid to equity shareholders following those to preference shareholders.

3. Differential Voting Right (DVR) shares

Investors in DVRs have fewer voting options than investors in equities. Companies give additional dividends to DVR shareholders in order to decrease voting rights. DVR stock prices are low since it has fewer voting rights. The price difference between stock shares and DVR shares is roughly 30–40%.

Chapter 1.4: Difference Between Share and Stock

According to Section 61 of the Companies Act of 2013, a corporation may convert fully paid-up shares of stock. The smallest unit into which the company's capital is divided, known as a "Share," signifies the ownership of the company's shareholders. On the other hand, a "Stock" is a group of fully paid-up shares of a member. When shares are converted to stock, the shareholder changes his or her status from shareholder to the stockholder, who has the same rights regarding dividends.

While the denomination of stock varies, all shares have the same denomination. One who wants to invest in shares must understand the distinction between shares and stock, as well as the circumstances under which shares can be changed into stock. Read the Chapter to see how we covered both of these concepts in detail.

Basis For Comparison	Share	Stock
Meaning	Small units, generally referred to as shares, make up a company's capital.	Stock refers to the transfer of a member's fully paid-up shares into a single fund.

Does a business have the ability to create original issues?	Yes	No
Paid up value	Shares may be paid up in full or in part.	Stock can only be paid for in whole.
Definite number	A share has a unique number that is a known quantity.	Such a number does not exist for stocks.
Fractional transfer	Not possible.	Possible
Nominal value	Yes	No
Denomination	Equal amounts	Unequal amounts

Chapter 1.5: Stockholders and equity ownership

The corporation owns the company's assets, while investors own the company's shares. So, if you hold 30% of a company's stock, stating that you own one-third of the stock is inaccurate; instead, mention that you own 100% of the company's shares. Shareholders are not free to do anything they want with a company's assets. A shareholder cannot take a chair since it belongs to the corporation, not the shareholder. Possession of the means of production "separation" means there is a break in joint ownership and control.

If you own stock, you can vote at shareholder meetings, receive dividends (the company's earnings) when and if they are distributed, and sell your shares to another individual. Furthermore, when you control a majority of a company's shares, your voting power grows, allowing you to influence its fate by indirectly picking its board of directors.

Most typical investors aren't concerned about the company's failure to govern. Being a shareholder is important because you are entitled to a percentage of the company's earnings, which, as we shall see, are the foundation of a stock's worth. As your stake in the company grows, so does your profit share. Many shares, on the other hand, do not pay dividends and instead reinvest earnings in the company's growth. Retained earnings, on the other hand, continue to reflect the value of a stock.

Chapter 1.6: The Stock Exchange Market Participants

As previously stated, a stock market is a marketplace where investors may purchase and sell stock investments, or ownership shares in a publicly listed company.

The stock market is a secondary capital market for buying and selling equity shares of publicly traded companies that are listed on recognized stock exchanges such as the London Stock Exchange, the NYSE/NASDAQ in the United States, and so on.

When a firm needs to generate cash, it selects the Initial Public Offering (IPO) (IPO). It reduces its holdings by selling equity shares on a recognized stock exchange, a procedure called Primary Capital Market. People who missed out on purchasing the shares during the initial public offering may now be able to do so now that they have been listed on stock exchanges (IPO). These individuals can now purchase shares from those who purchased them at the IPO on the secondary market.

The number of shares held by a person in relation to the total number of outstanding shares determines ownership. For example, if a firm has 1,000 outstanding shares of stock and one individual owns 300 of them, we say that person owns and has a claim to 30% of the corporation's assets and revenues. This is due to the fact that investors do not own the company; rather, they own its shares. Companies, on the other hand, are afforded special status by the law since they are considered legal entities.

To put it another way, companies may file taxes, borrow money, own property, be sued, and so on. When a company is called a "person," it implies that it owns its assets. A corporate office with chairs and tables is owned by the business, not the investors.

So, let's wrap up this portion with a little explanation. A stock market is a place where investors and traders buy and sell stock/shares, similar to how individuals buy and sell items [beef, beverages, fruits]. Stock/shares are bought and sold on two distinct exchanges. A corporation's stock/shares are sold in the primary market to institutions or significant investors such as banks, rich individuals, and other enterprises. The secondary market, which includes exchanges such as the NYSE, LSE, and others, is where institutions sell their shares in bulk or to merchants such as regular people and other significant investors.

Market Participants

The SEC's objective includes "maintaining standards for fair, orderly, and efficient markets." In order to accomplish this, the SEC controls a variety of securities market players. These are some examples:

- **Broker-Dealers** - Broker-dealers charge a fee to handle securities trades between buyers and sellers. A broker-dealer may purchase securities from a customer who is selling or sell securities from its own inventory to a customer who is buying.

- **Clearing Agencies** - Clearing Agencies are Self-Regulatory Organizations (SROs) that must register with the Securities and Exchange Commission (SEC). They, like other SROs, are in charge of writing, enforcing, and punishing members. Clearing agencies are classified into two types: clearing companies and depositories.

  o Clearing organizations, such as the National Securities Clearing Corporation (NSCC) and the Fixed Income Clearing Corporation (FICC), analyze member transactions, clear those trades, and provide automatic settlement instructions for those trades. Clearing corporations frequently serve as mediators in securities settlements.

- o Depositories, namely The Depository Trust Company (DTC), retain securities certificates for their participants, transfer holdings between them, and keep ownership records.

- **Credit Rating Agencies** - Credit Rating Agencies give comments on a company's or security's creditworthiness. A grade is used to indicate credit quality. Credit ratings often differentiate between investment grade and non-investment grade. A credit rating agency, for example, may issue a "triple A" credit rating as its top "investment grade" rating for corporate bonds, and a "double B" credit rating or below for "non-investment grade" or "high-yield" corporate bonds. Credit rating organizations that are registered with the SEC as such are referred to as "Nationally Recognized Statistical Rating Organizations."

- **ATSs** - An Alternative Trading System (ATS) is a trading system that fulfills the federal securities laws' definition of "exchange" but is not needed to register as a national securities exchange if it operates under the exemption afforded by Exchange Act Rule 3a1-1 (a). To be eligible for this exemption, an ATS must meet the conditions outlined in Rules 300-303 of Regulation ATS, which includes registering as a broker-dealer. ATSs that trade NMS stocks ("NMS Stock ATSs") must publicly file an initial Form ATS-N, revisions to the initial Form ATS-N, and notices of suspension of operations with the Commission. Form ATS-N mandates disclosures concerning the NMS Stock ATS's operations and the broker-dealer operator's and its affiliates ATS-related actions, among other things.

- **Investment Advisers** - Investment advisors are individuals or businesses who provide investment advice to investors or issue reports or analyses on securities. They engage in these activities in order to get compensated.

- **Securities Exchanges** - Securities exchanges are marketplaces for the purchase and sale of securities. There are now fifteen national securities exchanges registered with the SEC, including NYSE Euronext, NASDAQ, The Chicago Board Options Exchange, and BATS Exchange. SROs include stock exchanges.

- **Self-Regulatory Organizations (SROs)** - An SRO governs its industry by establishing regulations that control the behavior of its members. SROs also enforce the regulations they establish and sanction members who break them. The Financial Industry Regulatory Authority (FINRA) and the Municipal Securities Rulemaking Board are two well-known SROs (MSRB). The largest SRO in the securities business is FINRA. It is the primary broker-dealer regulator. The MSRB develops rules that govern municipal securities dealers. The SEC is in charge of both FINRA and the MSRB. Other SROs include clearing houses and stock exchanges.

- **Transfer Agents** -Transfer agents record changes in security ownership, keep security holder data for the issuer, revoke and issue certificates, and distribute dividends. Transfer

11

agents serve as intermediaries between issuing firms and securities holders. Transfer agents must be registered with the SEC or a bank regulatory organization if they are banks. Transfer agents are not governed by any SRO. The Securities and Exchange Commission (SEC) has issued rules and regulations for all licensed transfer agents. The goal is to assist in the timely and accurate clearing and settlement of securities transactions while also ensuring the security of securities and cash.

Chapter 1.7: How People Earn Money from Stocks & Shares

It may seem simple to some people to profit from the equity market by purchasing shares of companies listed on stock exchanges like the BSE or NSE. After all, anyone may purchase shares with a single click. Actually not at all. To profit from the stock market, one must develop a portfolio of shares that can consistently produce a respectable return over a lengthy period of time. The truth is that not everyone will be comfortable investing directly in the stock market because equity has traditionally been a volatile asset type with no assurance of returns. The one bright spot is that, among all asset classes, equity has been able to produce larger returns over longer periods of time than those adjusted for inflation. We start by examining the process of making money by purchasing shares. Dividends and capital appreciation are the two main avenues for profiting from shares.

Profits from capital growth: If one invests in shares, they can expect to profit from capital appreciation, or gains on their initial investment (principal) when the share price increases. The earnings or gains from stock might be as high as 100% or more. Though there is no assurance of capital growth. There is always a chance that market prices will stay below the buy price.

Receiving dividend income: Investors may anticipate income in the form of dividends in addition to capital gains on their shareholdings. When a firm declares partial or full dividends, it distributes its profits to its shareholders. Most of the time, the business only shares a portion of its revenues, keeping the remainder for other uses, like growth. Per share, dividends are paid out. It is referred to as 100 percent dividends if a corporation decides to distribute $10 per share with a $10 face value for each share.

Chapter 02: Learn About Trading Markets

Chapter 2.1: What is an Investment

An investment is a purchase made with the intent of generating income or appreciation. The phrase "appreciation" refers to the growth in the monetary value of an asset over time. When someone invests, the goal is to utilize the money to create wealth in the future, not to spend it. For example, an investor may buy a monetary asset today with the expectation that it would provide income or that it will be sold for a profit at a higher price tomorrow.

Many people believe that investing is similar to gambling, however, this is not the case. When you invest with the proper understanding, you will see the distinction between gambling and investing in the next part.

What Is the Difference Between an Investment and a Bet or Gamble?

You are transferring cash to individuals or businesses in the form of investment to be utilized to expand a firm, launch new projects, or support day-to-day income generation. While investments are hazardous, the expected return is favorable. Gambling, on the other hand, is more concerned with chance than with putting money to use. As a result, gambling is exceedingly dangerous and, in most cases, has a negative expected return. You may be wondering why you should invest when you can save money without taking any risks.

Investing, as previously said, puts money to work in order to improve its worth. When you buy stock or bonds, you place your money in the hands of a firm and its management team. While there is some uncertainty, the expected positive investment in capital appreciation, dividends, and interest payments more than compensates. Cash, on the other hand, would lose buying power owing to inflation and would not appreciate in value over time.

Chapter 2.2: The Types of Stock To Buy

The most frequent investing alternatives include stocks, bonds, and CDs. CDs and bonds are debt investments in which the borrower puts money into a project that is expected to create greater cash flow than the investors' interest.

Other investments include real estate and fixed-income securities.

This course will concentrate on stock/shares, but before we get into a stock investment, let's look at some stock selection recommendations.

Common stock and preferred stock

The majority of stock that people invest in is common stock. Common stock is a component of a corporation's ownership, with stockholders entitled to a proportionate part of any leftover assets if the company is dissolved. Shareholders of common stock have potentially infinite upside potential, but they also risk losing everything if the firm fails with no assets remaining.

Preferred stock differs from ordinary stock in that preferred stockholders are guaranteed a higher payout upon the company's dissolution. When it comes to dividend payments, preferred shareholders have first dibs, just before common shareholders. Therefore, preferred stock more closely resembles investments in fixed-income bonds than ordinary stock does. It is typical for a company to sell just common stock. Since this is what the majority of investors like to purchase, it makes sense.

Large-cap, mid-cap, and small-cap stocks

Market capitalization, the total value of a company's shares, is another metric used to classify stocks. Large-cap stocks are those with the largest market capitalizations, while mid-and small-cap stocks represent companies with intermediate and modest share values.

There seems to be no clear demarcation between the two categories. However, one common criterion is that large-cap stocks are those with a market valuation of $10 billion or more, while small-size stocks are those with a cap between $2 billion and $10 billion. Large-cap companies have market caps of over $10 billion and mid-cap stocks of over $2 billion, while small-cap stocks have market caps of less than $2 billion.

Stocks of mid- and small-cap firms have greater growth potential but are riskier investments, whereas those of large corporations are seen as safer bets by many investors. However, just because two companies are grouped together here doesn't mean they are necessarily good investment options or will have comparable future performance.

Domestic stocks and international stocks

You may categorize stocks depending on where they're located. Domestic U.S. shares may be distinguished from foreign equities by their focus on the location of the company's official headquarters.

It is important to keep in mind, nevertheless, that a stock's geographical classification may not correspond with the geographic origin of its sales.

One such company is Philip Morris International (NYSE: PM), whose headquarters are in the US but which only sells tobacco and other products outside the US. Business activities and financial data may not always make it clear whether or not a firm is really local or foreign. This is especially true of large international corporations.

Growth stocks and value stocks

Another form of classification differentiates between two common approaches to financial investment. Investors that focus on growth aim to find firms that are both successful and growing. When making investment decisions, value investors choose companies whose stock price is low in relation to that of their competitors or to the stock price of the company being invested in at the time.

Growth stocks have a higher degree of risk, but their potential rewards might be more enticing. Businesses that tap into strong and rising consumer demand, especially in combination with longer-term social shifts that promote the use of their goods and services, are more likely to be successful growth stocks. But competitors may be formidable, and if they manage to rile investors, a growth stock business can quickly lose its luster. When investors worry that growth may slow significantly over the long term, prices might drop precipitously, even if it has just slowed.

However, value stocks have a reputation for being more stable investments. They tend to be large, well-known companies that have already become industry leaders and have limited room to grow. Nevertheless, with stable corporate structures that have endured the test of time, they may be appealing choices for those seeking more pricing stability while preserving some of the advantages of stock exposure.

IPO stocks

To put it simply, IPO stocks are the shares of a business that has recently made its first public offering. Investors that want to get in on the ground floor of a viable company idea often show a lot of interest in initial public offerings (IPOs). However, they may be risky, especially if investors are divided on the prospects for growth and profit. Typically, a stock is regarded as an

IPO stock for at least a year, and often for as long as two to four years after it first begins trading to the public.

Dividend stocks and non-dividend stocks

Dividends are payments made on a regular basis to owners of several equities. Stocks that pay dividends are popular among investors because they provide a steady stream of income. Shares of any company that pays a dividend, even if it's just $0.01, are considered dividend stocks.

However, stocks do not need dividends. Investments in equities that do not pay dividends may nevertheless be worthwhile if their prices rise over time. In recent years, the trend has been toward more shares paying dividends to owners, yet some of the world's largest corporations still do not pay dividends.

Income stocks

Since most equities provide earnings to shareholders in the form of dividends, the two terms are sometimes used interchangeably. However, the phrase "income stocks" may also be used to describe the stocks of companies whose business models are more established and which have less room for future growth. Due to its suitability for cautious investors who need to withdraw income from their investment portfolios quickly, income stocks are particularly popular among retirees.

Cyclical stocks and non-cyclical stocks

National economies often grow and shrink in cycles, experiencing both prosperous and difficult times. Investors refer to the stocks of companies that are especially susceptible to broad economic cycles as "cyclical equities."

Companies in the manufacturing, tourism, and luxury goods industries are included in cyclical stocks since a slowdown in the economy might diminish the purchasing power of consumers. But when demand is high, as it often is when the economy is doing well, these companies may see rapid growth.

Non-cyclical companies, often known as defensive or secular stocks, do not experience significant demand swings. Companies like supermarket chains are non-cyclical because people will always need to eat, regardless of the state of the economy. There are times when non-cyclical corporations do better than the market, and times when cyclical equities do better than the market.

16

Safe stocks

The share prices of safe stocks tend to fluctuate less than the market as a whole. Low-volatility equities, often known as safe stocks, tend to be associated with sectors that are less sensitive to economic fluctuations. They also often provide dividends, which may be used to cushion the blow of falling share prices in volatile markets.

Stocks categorized by sector

Companies' stocks are often categorized according to the industry they operate in. The most popular basic groupings are stock market sectors.

- **Communication Services** -- Companies in the telephone, internet, media, and entertainment industries

- **Consumer Discretionary** -- retailers, automakers, and hotel and restaurant companies

- **Consumer Staples** -- food, beverage, tobacco, and household and personal products companies

- **Energy** -- oil and gas exploration and production companies, pipeline providers, and gas station operators

- **Financial** -- banks, mortgage finance specialists, and insurance and brokerage companies

- **Healthcare** -- health insurers, drug and biotech companies, and medical device makers

- **Industrial** -- airline, aerospace and defense, construction, logistics, machinery, and railroad companies

- **Materials** -- mining, forest products, construction materials, packaging, and chemical companies

- **Real Estate** -- real estate investment trusts and real estate management and development companies

- **Technology** -- hardware, software, semiconductor, communications equipment, and IT services companies

- **Utilities** -- electric, natural gas, water, renewable energy, and multi-product utility companies

Chapter 2.3: Stock Trading vs. Investing

When you trade stocks, you purchase and sell them regularly for a short-term profit, focusing on share prices. Investing is essentially the purchase of stocks in order to benefit from them over time. Following your investment education, you'll move on to stock trading in the next class.

Stock volatility

To invest in or trade stocks, you must first understand volatility. Volatility refers to the rate at which the price of a stock rises or decreases over a given period. More volatility in stock prices typically correlates to more risk and supports an investor in forecasting future changes.

While there is some danger in investing in the stock market, with the correct investment strategy, it can be done securely and with a minimal probability of long-term losses. Day traders, who buy and sell stocks quickly in response to market changes, are often more experienced. Long-term stock market investment, on the other hand, has shown to be a profitable method of creating wealth and is accessible to anybody.

Volatile stock in the market today

At this point, you should be introduced to a platform that allows you to view stock prices and activities in real time. We will be utilizing Yahoo Finance for this course, but there are various more sites where you can examine price movements.

Please take a minute to experiment with the platform and learn how it works; it is rather straightforward, and this course will aid you in understanding the technical aspects.

Create an account at www.finance.yahoo.com.

Now that you've explored the site, click the link below to see today's most recently added stock. https://finance.yahoo.com/u/yahoo-finance/watchlists/most-added

A snapshot of the most added stock while writing this course is shown below.

28 Symbols

Symbol	Company Name	Last Price	Change	% Change	Market Time	Volume	Avg Vol (3 month)	Market Cap
AAPL	Apple Inc.	155.09	+4.47	+2.97%	4:00 PM EDT	89.23M	94.61M	2,600.05B
MSFT	Microsoft Corporation	287.15	+10.71	+3.87%	4:00 PM EDT	34.25M	37.44M	2,180.99B
GOOGL	Alphabet Inc.	2583.96	+64.94	+2.58%	4:00 PM EDT	1.55M	1.91M	1,764.99B
GOOG	Alphabet Inc.	2593.21	+58.39	+2.30%	4:00 PM EDT	1.51M	1.54M	1,760.27B
AMZN	Amazon.com, Inc.	2947.33	+110.27	+3.89%	4:00 PM EDT	3.61M	3.81M	1,538.55B
TSLA	Tesla, Inc.	801.89	+35.52	+4.63%	4:00 PM EDT	22.28M	26.39M	860.10B
BRK-B	Berkshire Hathaway Inc.	332.55	+2.57	+0.78%	4:02 PM EDT	6.53M	5.25M	728.73B
NVDA	NVIDIA Corporation	229.73	+16.43	+7.70%	4:00 PM EDT	48.22M	50.46M	572.49B
FB	Meta Platforms, Inc.	192.03	+5.40	+2.89%	4:00 PM EDT	31.72M	34.58M	525.44B
JPM	JPMorgan Chase & Co.	132.48	+2.31	+1.77%	4:00 PM EDT	14.79M	16.48M	391.19B
DIS	The Walt Disney Company	134.2	+5.17	+4.01%	4:03 PM EDT	9.52M	12.21M	249.48B
BABA	Alibaba Group Holding Limited	76.76	-1.00	-1.29%	4:01 PM EDT	85.16M	24.56M	246.34B
NKE	NIKE, Inc.	119.4	+1.83	+1.56%	4:00 PM EDT	9.82M	6.58M	196.93B
INTC	Intel Corporation	44.81	+0.41	+0.92%	4:00 PM EDT	34.45M	38.85M	188.34B
AMD	Advanced Micro Devices, Inc.	109.33	+7.08	+6.92%	4:00 PM EDT	112.30M	93.80M	181.47B
NFLX	Netflix, Inc.	343.75	+12.74	+3.85%	4:00 PM EDT	4.94M	7.92M	156.90B
LMT	Lockheed Martin Corporation	448.67	+4.22	+0.95%	4:03 PM EDT	1.75M	2.36M	122.18B
PYPL	PayPal Holdings, Inc.	100.46	+3.59	+3.71%	4:00 PM EDT	17.11M	21.26M	117.04B
F	Ford Motor Company	16.06	+0.32	+2.03%	4:02 PM EDT	64.77M	104.61M	65.53B
MRNA	Moderna, Inc.	148.12	-1.95	-1.30%	4:00 PM EDT	13.19M	8.92M	59.70B
SNOW	Snowflake Inc.	170.78	+4.03	+2.42%	4:00 PM EDT	8.11M	4.73M	56.60B
OXY	Occidental Petroleum Corporation	54.53	-1.06	-1.91%	4:00 PM EDT	49.14M	28.79M	50.93B
NIO	NIO Inc.	14.93	+0.83	+5.89%	4:02 PM EDT	138.77M	60.75M	31.23B
PARA	Paramount Global	35.21	-0.56	-1.57%	4:00 PM EDT	13.14M	15.69M	21.40B
ZIM	ZIM Integrated Shipping Services Ltd.	85.24	+2.70	+3.27%	4:00 PM EDT	8.23M	3.80M	10.21B
UPST	Upstart Holdings, Inc.	97.48	+8.14	+9.11%	4:00 PM EDT	17.65M	9.29M	9.18B
SOFI	SoFi Technologies, Inc.	8.2	+0.27	+3.40%	4:00 PM EDT	52.32M	61.68M	6.56B
COUP	Coupa Software Incorporated	72.55	-17.27	-19.23%	4:00 PM EDT	24.56M	2.14M	5.99B

19

Chapter 2.4: Opening A Trading Account

It may appear that choosing the right Demat and trading account is a difficult undertaking, but it does not have to be. You should be able to identify the best online stock broker by first deciding what type of account you want and then comparing several online stock brokers.

Here's how to establish a trading account step by step:

1. Determine the type of demat trading account you will require.

What are your long-term investment objectives? If you simply want to invest for a specific extremely short-term reason and don't want your money tied up until you retire, a conventional brokerage account is a way to go. If you utilize these accounts, you may have to pay tax on investment income and dividends, but you may take your money whenever you like.

2. Analyze the various choices' costs and benefits.

Almost all of the major discount brokers now provide no-commission trading. They may also offer you a discount if you do something particular, such as transfer a large investment account from another broker. However, it is critical to review each online brokerage firm's whole price schedule, especially if you want to trade anything other than stocks, since they may have their own costs.

3. Consider the amenities and services available

It's not only about the price, especially for new investors. Of course, obtaining the lowest price is the best option if all other elements are equal, but there are a few other aspects to consider when selecting a broker:

4. Fill out the trading account application form.

You may open a new trading account with an online broker by filling out an online application, which is normally a quick and simple process. Your PAN card and other identifying details will be requested. If you want to pursue margin privileges or the right to trade options, you'll need to sign additional paperwork, and the broker will need to know about your net value, employment standing, available assets, and anticipated returns on those assets.

5. Put money into your trading account.

Your new online broker will most likely give you a variety of options for funding your demat trading account. While opening your new account, keep your broker's minimums in mind. Many banks have different minimum requirements for taxable and retirement accounts, as well as different minimum requirements for margin accounts.

Chapter 2.5: Learn How To Start Trading

When you get your mind straight, you can begin learning to trade by following these five fundamental stages.

1. Open a Trading Account

Sorry if it appears like we are repeating ourselves, but you never know! (Remember the person who did everything but connect to his new computer?) Open a stock brokerage account with a reputable online stock broker. Even if you already have a personal account, it is a good idea to have a professional trading account separate. Learn how to use the account interface and take use of the free trading tools and research available only to customers. Virtual trading is available from a variety of firms. Some websites, such as Investopedia, also provide online broker reviews to assist you in finding the correct broker.

2. Learn to Read: A Market Crash Course

Financial publications, books on the stock market, internet courses, and so forth. There is a multitude of information available, much of it for free. Avoid narrowing your attention to just one aspect of the trading game. Instead, research anything market-related, including ideas and notions you don't think are particularly important right now. Trading sets off on a trip that frequently leads to an unexpected destination. Even if you believe you know precisely where you're heading right now, your wide and deep market knowledge will come in handy again and again.

The following are five books that every new trader should read:

1. *Stock Market Wizards* by Jack D. Schwager[1]

2. *Trading for a Living* by Dr. Alexander Elder[2]

3. *John Murphy's Technical Analysis of Financial Markets 3*

4. *Martin Zweig4's Winning on Wall Street*

5. *The Nature of Risk* by Justin Mamis[5]

Begin following the market in your leisure time every day. Get up early and learn about overnight price movements in foreign exchange markets. (A few decades ago, US traders didn't have to monitor worldwide markets, but that's all changed because to ofe rapid expansion of computerized trading and derivative products that connect equities, FX, and bond markets around the world.)

Yahoo Finance, Google Finance, and CBS MoneyWatch are excellent resources for beginner investors. Look no further than The Wall Street Journal and Bloomberg for more expert coverage.

3. Learn to Analyze

Examine hundreds of price charts across various periods to learn the principles of technical analysis. Fundamental research may appear to give a better road to profits since it analyzes growth curves and income streams, but traders live and die by a market movement that deviates significantly from underlying fundamentals. Continue to examine firm spreadsheets since they provide a trading advantage over those who disregard them. They will, however, not help you survive your first year as a trader.

Your knowledge of charts and technical analysis has now led you into the mystical domain of price prediction. Securities can only move up or down, promoting a long-side trade or a short sell. Prices, in actuality, may do a variety of things, such as chop sideways for weeks at a time or whipsaw rapidly in both directions, shaking off buyers and sellers.

The temporal horizon becomes quite important at this stage. Financial markets churn out fractal trends and trading ranges that create separate price movements at short-, intermediate-, and long-term intervals. This indicates that a security or index might form a long-term uptrend, an intermediate decline, and a short-term trading range all at once. Most trading chances will emerge from interactions between these time periods, rather than complicating the forecast.

Buying the dip is a typical example, with traders entering a strong rally when the market sells off in a shorter period. Looking at each security in three-time frames, beginning with 60-minute, daily, and weekly charts is the greatest approach to assess this three-dimensional playing field.

4. Practice Trading

It's now time to test the waters without jeopardizing your trading position. Paper trading, also known as virtual trading, is an ideal alternative, allowing the novice to monitor real-time market movement and make purchasing and selling decisions that form the foundation of a theoretical performance record. It usually requires using a stock market simulator to simulate the behavior of a genuine stock exchange. Make several transactions with varying holding durations and techniques, and then examine the outcomes for obvious problems.

Investopedia offers a free stock market game, and many firms also allow clients to practice paper trading with their real money entry systems. This has the added benefit of teaching the software so that you don't inadvertently hit the wrong buttons while messing around with family money.

So, when do you make the leap and begin trading for real money? There is no ideal answer since simulated trading has a weakness that will most certainly show up when you start trading for real, even if your paper results appear great.

Traders must balance the competing feelings of greed and fear. Paper trading does not elicit these feelings, which can only be felt via genuine profit and loss. In fact, this psychological factor disqualifies more first-year players than poor decision-making. Your first actions as a novice trader must acknowledge this obstacle and handle any leftover money and self-worth concerns.

5. Other Methods for Learning and Practicing Trading

Though experience is a great instructor, don't overlook more education as you advance in your trading profession. Classes, whether online or in-person, may be beneficial, and they range in complexity from novice (for example, training on how to study the aforementioned analytic charts) to pro. More specialized seminars, sometimes led by a professional trader, can give significant insight into the market as a whole as well as particular investing methods. Most concentrate on one sort of asset, one facet of the market, or one trading approach. Some may be intellectual in nature, while others are more akin to workshops in which you actively take positions, test entrance, and exit tactics, and participate in other activities (often with a simulator).

Putting time and money into research and analysis might be educational and useful. Some investors may find it more advantageous to watch or observe market pros than to try to apply newly learnt principles themselves. There are several paid subscription sites accessible on the internet: Investors.com and Morningstar are two well-known businesses.

It's also a good idea to find a mentor—a hands-on coach who can train you, analyze your technique, and provide advice. If you don't know any personally, you may always purchase one. As part of their ongoing education offerings, several online trading schools also provide mentoring to their students.

Chapter 2.6: Learn About The Best Trading Platforms

The stock trading 2.0 course is for you if you want to become a more advanced stock trader. The advanced course will go further into stock market principles, finding the best stock, and more sophisticated trading tactics. You will also learn more about RSI, MA, and how to interpret market news like a pro.

However, let us return to today's business; the following is a list of the greatest trading platforms available today.

Fidelity

Fidelity

With no trading costs, over 3,700 no-transaction-fee mutual funds, and an excellent research and trading interface, Fidelity Investments is an excellent place to invest. One of the numerous advantages of this organization is its capacity to supply no-fee index funds and a good customer service record.

Pros

• Commission-free stock, ETF, and options trading; a wide range of research providers.

• Excellent client service.

• Index funds with no expense ratio.

• App that has received a lot of favorable reviews.

Cons

• Broker-assisted trading is rather expensive.

E✳TRADE

E*TRADE

E*TRADE has long been renowned as one of the most recognizable online brokerage organizations. Active traders will appreciate the company's zero-fee trading platforms, while novice investors will benefit from a comprehensive library of training materials.

Pros

• Tools that are simple to use.

• A diverse choice of investment possibilities; exceptional customer service; and access to extensive research

• Mobile app with advanced features.

• Trade stock, options, and ETFs without paying a commission.

• The site's design should be better.

MERRILL
A BANK OF AMERICA COMPANY

Merrill Edge

Merrill Edge offers exceptional customer service, substantial research, and low prices. Customers of parent company Bank of America will also appreciate the ingenious integration, which allows them to access both accounts with a single login.

Pros

• Comprehensive third-party research;

• Bank of America integration.

• Advanced investors may notice that there are fewer stocks accessible.

TD Ameritrade

TD Ameritrade

With improved trading tools, no fees on online stock and ETF trades, and a wide range of mutual funds, TD Ameritrade caters to both aggressive traders and inexperienced investors.

Pros

• Trade stock and ETFs without paying a commission.

• There is no charge for research.

• Trading platforms of the highest caliber.

• There is no account minimum.

• Excellent client service.

• A wide range of investing options.

Cons

• There are no fractional shares.

ally invest

Ally Invest

Ally Invest's extensive trading platform and a plethora of free research, charting, statistics, and analytical tools will appeal to active traders. It's also appropriate for beginning investors, who will like the lack of a minimum account balance and the lack of yearly fees.

Pros

• No account minimum; no commissions on qualifying US stocks, options, and ETFs; solid web-based platform; rich research and tools

Cons

• There are no no-transaction-fee mutual funds available, nor are there any branches.

Chapter 2.7: Most Made Investment Mistakes

Here are the seven most common investment blunders:

1. Not Understanding the Investment

Warren Buffett, one of the world's most successful investors, advises against investing in firms whose business strategies you don't comprehend. A diversified portfolio of ETFs or mutual funds may help you avoid this risk. Before you buy individual stocks, be sure you properly understand each firm that those stocks represent.

2. Falling in Love With a Company

When we watch a firm we've invested in succeed, it's all too tempting to fall in love with it and forget that we purchased the shares as an investment. Remember, you bought this stock to earn money. If any of the factors that led you to purchase shares in the company suddenly alter, you may want to consider selling.

3. Lack of Patience

In the long run, a cautious and steady approach to portfolio expansion will produce higher returns. Expecting a portfolio to fulfill duties for which it was not designed is a recipe for catastrophe. This implies you should keep your expectations for portfolio growth and returns as reasonable as possible.

4. Too Much Investment Turnover

Another return killer is turnover, or often changing positions. Unless you're an institutional investor who can take advantage of low commission rates, transaction expenses may eat you alive—not to mention the short-term tax rates and the opportunity cost of missing out on other sensible investments' long-term advantages

5. Attempting to Time the Market

Attempting to time the market also reduces rewards. It is extremely difficult to correctly time the market. Even institutional investors frequently fail to succeed. Gary P. Brinson, L. Randolph Hood, and Gilbert L. Beebower published a well-known research on the "Determinants Of Portfolio Performance" (Financial Analysts Journal, 1986). This analysis found that investment policy decisions explained roughly 94 percent of the variation in returns across time. 1 In layman's words, this suggests that the majority of a portfolio's performance can be explained by asset allocation decisions rather than timing or securities selection.

6. Waiting to Get Even

Getting even is merely another technique to ensure that any profit you have accumulated is lost. It suggests you're holding off on selling a loss until it returns to its original cost base. In behavioral finance, this is referred to as a "cognitive error." Investors lose in two ways when they fail to recognize a loss. To begin, they avoid selling a loser, which may continue to fall in value until it is worthless. Second, there is the potential cost of putting those investment resources to greater use.

7. Failing to Diversify

Professional investors may be able to produce alpha (or excess return over a benchmark) by investing in a few concentrated positions, but average investors should avoid doing so. It is better to follow the diversification concept. It is vital to have exposure to all major sectors when building an exchange-traded fund (ETF) or mutual fund portfolio. Include all important sectors while constructing an individual stock portfolio. As a general rule, don't put more than 5% to 10% of your money into any single investment.

Chapter 2.8: The Intelligent Investor And Example of Them
Personality Traits of the Best Investors

Successful stock market investors have certain characteristics. The more your personal style resembles the greats, the more likely you are to make money. These effective attributes include patience, dedication, and conducting thorough research on your assets.

Patience

Above and beyond all other characteristics, your level of patience will have an influence on your end outcomes. Perhaps this is due to the fact that patience is the polar opposite of the profit-killing emotions that afflict most investors, such as impatience, greed, and fear.

In fact, a calm hand will typically remove any stock market blunders caused by impatience, wrath, or remorse. Patience equals profits in the world of investment.

Ability to Tune out Noise

This personality attribute will serve you well in a variety of situations, including the financial market, mainstream media, and even noisy children. With numerous distractions and advertising interruptions every day, how can anybody live unless they can ignore the commotion?

Even if we limit ourselves to the stock market, the torrent of data points and information is far from overwhelming. The better you can sort through all the confusing signals and opposing viewpoints, the higher your ultimate trading account balance will be. Don't give up; you'll discover that you get really good at these things pretty soon!

Staying the Course

Have you ever sold a stock only to see the price rise? Staying the course, like its close cousin "patience," should help you stay ahead of the pack.

To put it another way, trading more frequently does not always result in higher or better trading earnings. In fact, the frequency of trading is usually inversely proportional to earnings.

Calm in the Storm

When the sky is falling and people are crushing one another to get rid of their stocks, the investors who remain cool win. In fact, the calm and discerning among us will be able to see all of the overlooked possibilities that others would miss amid the rush.

Doing the Homework

Successful investors always learn rather than bet on views based on inadequate understanding. Most individuals base their choices on sound bites or fragments of argumentation. In contrast, the best stock market traders do their own research and learn until they know which investing movements will pay off. When they are unsure about a trading move, they learn more—until they know a lot and have a good comprehension of their options.

Asking for Knowledge

Great stock market investors understand what they don't know. They largely rely on the expertise and knowledge of experts and professionals.

They are also not afraid to ask questions, and they prefer to spend the time in the beginning gathering all of the data rather than learning after it is too late. To put it another way, they make certain that they are well-informed and well-prepared.

The beauty of all of these strong investor personality qualities is that you can easily mimic them right now. You don't have to be Superman or a trading troll in a dark basement with seven monitors—just put in the effort necessary to make intelligent decisions and remain cool even during market panics.

Examples of Intelligent Investors

Great money managers are the financial world's rock stars. The greatest investors have all amassed fortunes as a result of their success, and in many cases, they have assisted millions of others in achieving similar results.

These investors' trading tactics and mindsets range greatly; some developed fresh and novel ways to examine their assets, while others chose stocks almost exclusively on instinct. Where these investors agree is in their ability to routinely outperform the market.

Benjamin Graham

Ben Graham was an exceptional investment manager and financial instructor. He wrote two investing masterpieces of unequaled importance, among other things. He is also widely regarded as the founder of two important financial disciplines: security analysis and value investing.

The premise of Graham's value investing is that every investment should be worth significantly more than the amount paid for it by the investor. He believed in basic research and sought for firms with excellent balance sheets, little debt, above-average profit margins, and plenty of cash flow.

John Templeton

One of the twentieth century's best contrarians, John Templeton is claimed to have purchased low during the Depression, sold high during the Internet boom, and made a few excellent predictions in between. Templeton established some of the largest and most successful foreign investment funds in the world. He sold his Templeton funds to the Franklin Group in 1992. Money magazine dubbed him "probably the best worldwide stock picker of the century" in 1999. Templeton was knighted by Queen Elizabeth II for his various accomplishments as a naturalized British citizen residing in the Bahamas.

John Neff

Neff joined Wellington Management Co. in 1964 and lasted for more than 30 years, managing three of the company's funds. His favorite investment strategy was investing in prominent sectors via indirect routes, and he was regarded as a value investor since he focused on firms with low P/E ratios and high dividend yields. He managed the Windsor Fund for 31 years (finishing in 1995) and produced a return of 13.7 percent, compared to 10.6 percent for the S& P 500. This represents a gain of more than 53 times the initial investment in 1964.

Jesse Livermore

Jesse Livermore lacked formal education and no prior expertise in the stock market. He was a self-made man who learned from both his wins and losers. These wins and disappointments served to solidify trading notions that may still be found in the market today. Livermore began trading for himself in his early teens, and by the age of sixteen, he had allegedly made over $1,000, which was a lot of money back then. Over the following few years, he gained money by betting against so-called "bucket shops," which didn't process actual deals and instead let consumers gamble against the house on stock price swings.

Peter Lynch

From 1977 through 1990, Peter Lynch managed the Fidelity Magellan Fund, which raised its assets from $18 million to $14 billion. 4 More crucially, Lynch outperformed the S& P 500 Index benchmark in 11 of those 13 years, with a yearly average return of 29%. 56 Peter Lynch was often labeled as a chameleon because he adapted to whatever investing approach was working at the moment. When it came to selecting individual equities, however, Peter Lynch stayed with what he understood and/or could easily grasp.

Warren Buffett

Warren Buffett dubbed the "Oracle of Omaha," is widely regarded as one of the most successful investors in history.

Following Benjamin Graham's ideals, he acquired a multibillion-dollar fortune mostly via the purchase of stocks and companies through Berkshire Hathaway. A 1965 investor in Berkshire

Hathaway who put in $10,000 is today worth more than $165 million. 78 For decades, Buffett's investment strategy of discipline, patience, and value has consistently beaten the market.

Chapter 03: Trading Analysis For Beginners

Chapter 3.1: What Is Technical Analysis

Technical analysis is a trading discipline that uses statistical trends derived from trading activity, such as price movement and volume, to analyze investments and uncover trading opportunities. Technical analysis, as opposed to fundamental analysis, aims to assess the value of a security based on corporate performance such as sales and earnings.

Understanding Technical Analysis

Technical analysis methods are used to examine how supply and demand for securities affect price, volume, and implied volatility variations. It is based on the idea that, when supplemented with correct investing or trading criteria, a security's history trading activity and price variations can be effective indicators of the security's future price movements.

It is commonly used to generate short-term trading signals from various charting tools, but it may also be used to determine a security's strength or weakness in relation to the greater market or one of its sectors. This information helps analysts improve their overall valuation estimate.

Today's kind of technical analysis was developed by Charles Dow and the Dow Theory in the late 1800s. Several notable scholars, including William P. Dow Theory ideas, were added to by Hamilton, Robert Rhea, Edson Gould, and John Magee, contributing to the construction of its basis. Nowadays, technical analysis includes hundreds of patterns and signals created over many years of research.

Chapter 3.2: What Is Fundamental Analysis

Fundamental analysis (FA) is a way of determining the fundamental value of a security by evaluating associated economic and financial elements. Fundamental analysts research everything that has the potential to impact the value of a security, from macroeconomic issues like the state of the economy and industry circumstances to microeconomic components such as the effectiveness of the company's management

The end aim is to arrive at a figure that an investor may compare to the present price of an asset to determine whether it is cheap or overpriced.

This type of stock research is said to be in opposition to technical analysis, which anticipates price direction by analyzing previous market data such as price and volume.

Understanding Fundamental Analysis

All stock analysis aims to determine if a security's market value is correct. Fundamental research is often conducted from a macro to a micro level in order to uncover stocks that are not being valued appropriately by the market.

To arrive at a fair market valuation for the stock, analysts often examine the overall status of the economy, followed by the strength of the specific industry, before focusing on individual business performance.

Fundamental analysis uses publicly accessible data to determine the value of a stock or other type of investment. An investor, for example, can undertake fundamental research on the value of a bond by looking at economic variables such as interest rates and the overall status of the economy, then examining bond issuer information, such as potential changes in credit rating.

Fundamental analysis for equities examines sales, profits, future growth, return on equity, profit margins, and other statistics to estimate a company's underlying worth and future development potential. All of this information may be found in a company's financial statements.

Chapter 3.3: Put And Call Option

A derivative is a contract that grants the buyer the right, but not the responsibility, to purchase or sell the underlying asset by a defined date (expiration date) at a predetermined price (strike price). One may choose between a call option and a put option. American options can be exercised at any moment before they expire. Only on the expiration date may European options be exercised.

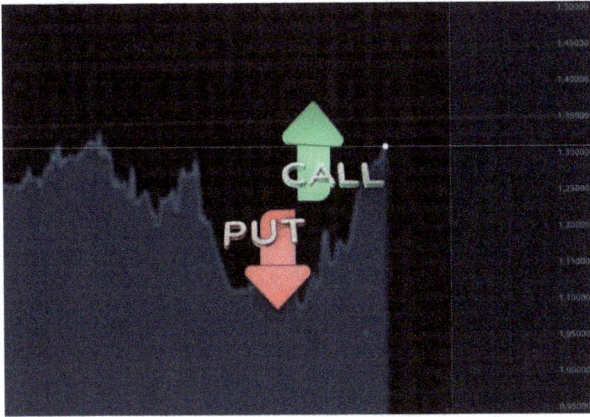

To enter into an option contract, the buyer must pay an option premium. Calls and puts are the two most frequent forms of options:

1. Call options

A call option buyer has the right, but not the obligation, to acquire the underlying asset at the strike price specified in the option contract. Investors buy calls when they believe the price of the underlying asset will rise and sell calls when they believe it will decline.

2. Put options

Puts allow the buyer the right, but not the responsibility, to sell the underlying asset at the contract's strike price. If the put buyer exercises their option, the writer (seller) of the put option is compelled to acquire the asset. Investors purchase puts when they expect the underlying asset's price will fall and sell options when they feel it will rise.

Payoffs for Options: Calls and Puts

Calls

The buyer of a call option pays the option premium in full at the time the contract is entered into. Following that, the buyer stands to earn if the market moves in his favor. There is no chance that the option will generate any further loss above the purchase price. One of the most tempting parts of purchasing alternatives is this. For a little investment, the buyer obtains a limitless profit potential with a known and tightly restricted loss.

If the underlying asset's spot price does not increase above the option strike price before the option expires, the investor loses the money paid for the option. However, if the underlying asset's price exceeds the strike price, the call buyer profits. Profit is calculated as the difference between the market price and the strike price of the option, multiplied by the added value of the underlying asset, less the cost of the option.

For instance, if you had a stock option for 100 shares, you'd get 100 shares of the underlying stock. So, let's say a trader invests in ABC stock by purchasing one call option contract at a $25 strike price. He spends $150 on the choice. On the expiration date of the option, ABC stock is selling for $35 a share. The option buyer/holder exercises his right to buy 100 shares of ABC at $25 per share (the option's strike price). He sells the shares immediately at the current market price of $35 a share.

He purchased $2,500 for 100 shares ($25 x 100) and sold them for $3,500 ($35 x 100). His option profit is $1,000 ($3,500 - $2,500), less the $150 premium paid for the option. Thus, removing transaction charges, his net profit is $850 ($1,000 - $150). That's a great return on investment (ROI) for only a $150 expenditure.

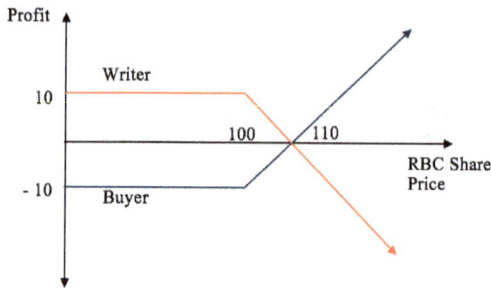

Puts

A put option grants the buyer the right to sell the underlying asset at the strike price of the option. The buyer's profit on the option is determined by how far the current price falls below the strike price. If the strike price is less than the spot price, the put buyer is "in the money." The option will expire unexercised if the current price remains greater than the strike price. The option buyer's loss is, once again, limited to the option price paid.

If the underlying asset's spot price is less than the strike price of the contract, the put writer is "out-of-the-money." Their loss is equivalent to the profit of the put option buyer. If the spot price remains above the contract's strike price, the option expires unexecuted, and the writer keeps the option premium.

Figure 2 depicts the payout for a hypothetical 3-month RBC put option with a $10 option premium and a $90 strike price. The possible loss for the buyer is limited to the amount of the put option contract ($10).

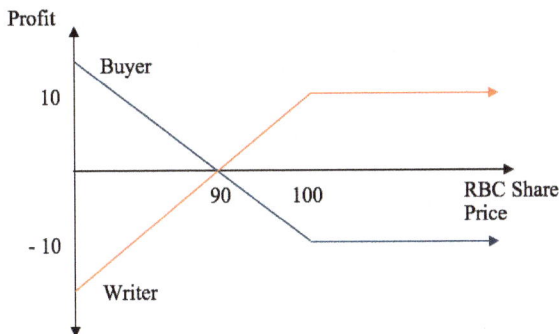

Chapter 3.4: Trade And Put Calls
Call-Buying Strategy

When you purchase a call option, you pay the option premium in return for the right to purchase shares at a defined price (strike price) on or before a specific date (expiration date). Because calls provide leverage, investors frequently purchase them when they are optimistic about a stock or other investment.

Assume ABC Company is valued at $50. The one-month at-the-money call option on the stock costs $3. Would you rather buy 100 ABC shares for $5,000 or one call option for $300 ($3 × 100 shares), with the payout based on the stock's closing price one month from now? Consider the visual representations of the two scenarios below.

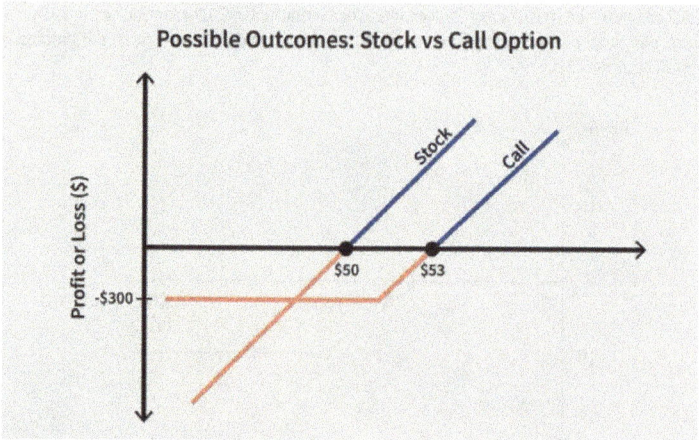

Possible Outcomes: Stock vs Call Option

Each investment, as you can see, has a different rate of return. While purchasing the stock will need a $5,000 investment, you may control an equivalent number of shares for only $300 by purchasing a call option. Also, the stock transaction has a breakeven price of $50 per share, but the option trade has a breakeven price of $53 per share (not factoring in commissions or fees).

While both assets have infinite upside potential in the month after purchase, the loss situations are radically different. For example, although the maximum potential loss on the option is $300, the maximum potential loss on the stock purchase is the whole $5,000 initial investment if the share price falls to zero.

Closing the Position

Investors can exit their call holdings by selling them back to the market or having them exercised, in which case they must pay the counterparty who sold them the calls in cash (and receive the shares in exchange).

Continuing with our example, suppose the stock was trading at $55 as the one-month expiry approached. Under these conditions, you might sell your call for around $500 ($5 × 100 shares), giving you a net profit of $200 ($500 less the $300 premium).

You might also have the call exercised, in which case you would be required to pay $5,000 ($50 × 100 shares) and the counterparty who sold you the call would deliver the shares. The profit with this method would likewise be $200 ($5,500 - $5,000 - $300 = $200). It is worth noting that the reward from exercising or selling the call is the same: a net profit of $200.

Call Option Considerations

Purchasing calls necessitates more considerations than purchasing the underlying stock. Assuming you've decided on the stock for which you want to purchase calls, here are some things to think about:

- **Amount of Premium Outlay**: This is the initial stage in the procedure. Because of the substantially smaller financial outlay for the call, most investors would prefer to buy a call than the underlying stock. Continuing with the previous example, if you have $1,500 to invest, you can only buy 30 ABC Co. shares at the current stock price of $50. However, based on the one-month call price of $3, you would be able to purchase five contracts (each contract controlling 100 shares and hence costing $300), implying that you have the right—but not the obligation—to purchase 500 shares at $50.

- **Strike price**: This is one of two major option variables to consider, the other being the time to expiry. Because the striking price has a significant influence on the success of an options trade, you should conduct some research to determine the best strike price. The basic rule for call options is that the lower the strike price, the bigger the call premium (because you obtain the right to buy the underlying stock at a lower price). The smaller the call premium, the more out-of-pocket the call. In this scenario, the strike price is at the money, or equal to the current stock price of $50.

- **Time to expiration**: This is still another important factor. All else being equal, the longer the period to expiry for options, the larger the option premium. Choosing an expiry date necessitates a balance between time and expense. Typically, options contracts expire on the third Friday of each month.

- **Number of options contracts**: The call premium will be determined after the strike price and the time to expiry have been determined. With $1,500 to invest and each one-month $50 call option costing $300, you must determine whether to buy five contracts for the whole amount or three or four contracts and retain some cash in reserve.

- **Type of option order**: Option prices, being a derivative of stock prices, may be highly volatile. You must select whether to put a market order or a limit order for your calls.

Chapter 3.5: Trading candlestick

Candlestick charts originated in Japan much before their Western counterparts, the bar chart, and the point-and-figure chart, both of which owe a great deal to that country's technological prowess. While there was a link between pricing and rice supply and demand in the 1700s, a

Japanese man named Homma observed that merchants' emotions had a big impact on the markets.

Candlesticks portray this sentiment graphically by utilizing different colors to represent the size of price fluctuations. Traders use candlesticks to make trading decisions based on regularly recurring patterns that help forecast the price's short-term direction.

Candlestick Components

A daily candlestick chart, like a bar chart, depicts the market's open, high, low, and closing values for the day. The "true body" of the candlestick is an important component of the candlestick.

This actual body represents the price range between the opening and closing of that day's transaction.

If the genuine body is filled in or black, the close was lower than the open. If the real body is empty, it means that the closure exceeded the open.

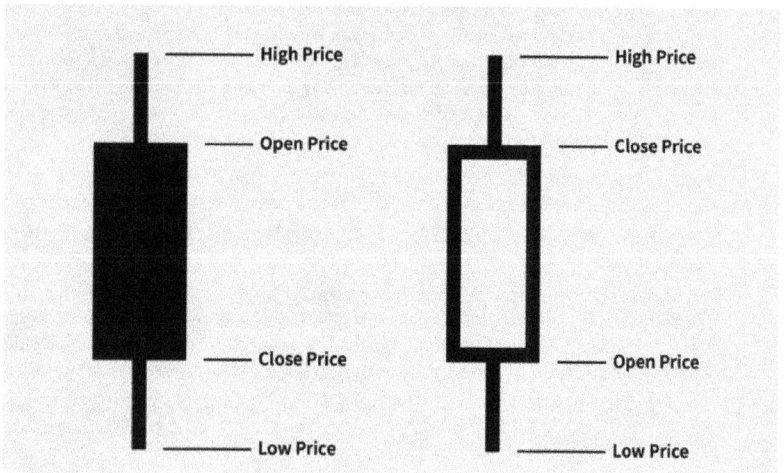

Basic Candlestick Patterns

Price movements that go up and down create candlesticks. Price movements might look random at times, but they can also generate patterns that traders can utilize for study or trading. There are several varieties of candlesticks to choose from. To get you started, I'll give you an example.

There are distinct bullish and bearish patterns. Bullish patterns predict that the price will rise, while bearish patterns predict that the price will decrease. Candlestick patterns depict price movement tendencies rather than assurances, and as such, they may not always work.

Bearish Engulfing Pattern

When sellers outweigh purchasers during an upswing, a bearish engulfing pattern forms. This movement is mirrored by a lengthy red real body devouring a little green genuine body. The trend suggests that sellers have recovered market power and that the price may continue to fall.

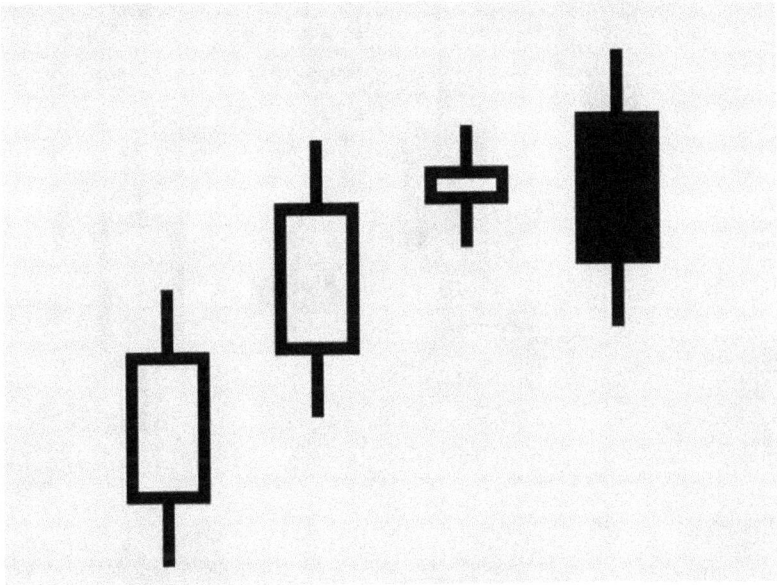

Bullish Engulfing Pattern

When buyers outweigh sellers on the bullish side of the market, an engulfing pattern forms. A lengthy green genuine body envelops a little red genuine body on the chart. Now that the bulls have reclaimed power, the price may rise.

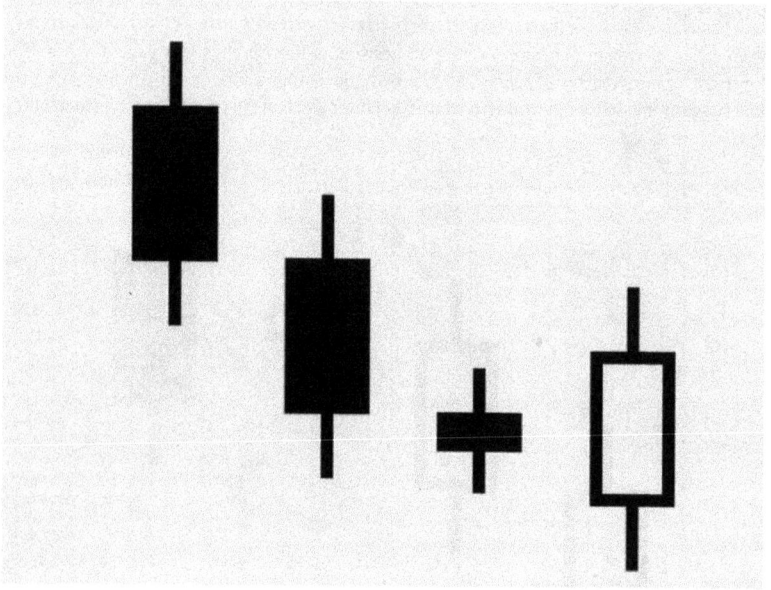

Bearish Evening Star

An evening star is a topping pattern. To be identified, the last candle in the pattern must open below the previous day's small genuine body. The small body might be red or green. The last candle closes deeply into the genuine body of the candle from two days ago. The pattern symbolizes the buyers waiting before the sellers take control. It is likely that more selling will occur. cur.

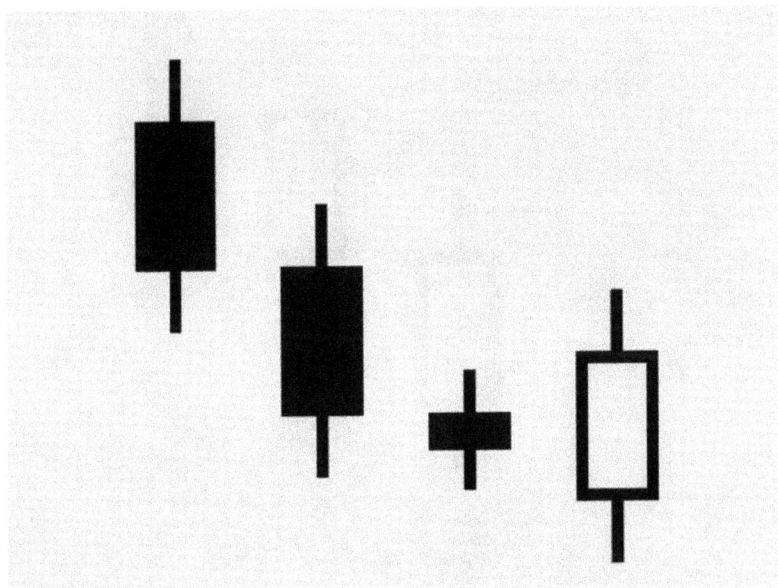

Bearish Harami

A bearish harami is a little genuine body (red) that has been entirely wrapped with the real body from the previous day. This isn't always a good idea, but it's worth mentioning. The pattern represents the clients' anxiety. If the price rises further, the uptrend may continue; however, a down candle after this pattern suggests that the decline will continue.

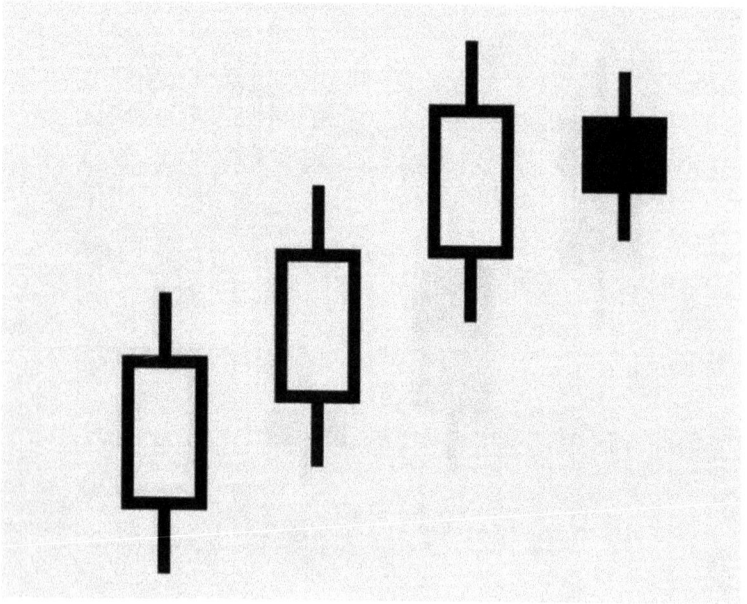

Bullish Harami

The bullish harami is the polar opposite of the upside-down negative harami. The impact is decreasing, with a little real body (green) appearing inside the previous day's large actual body (red). This alerts the technician to the fact that the trend is coming to an end. More gains may be on the way if this is followed by another rising day.

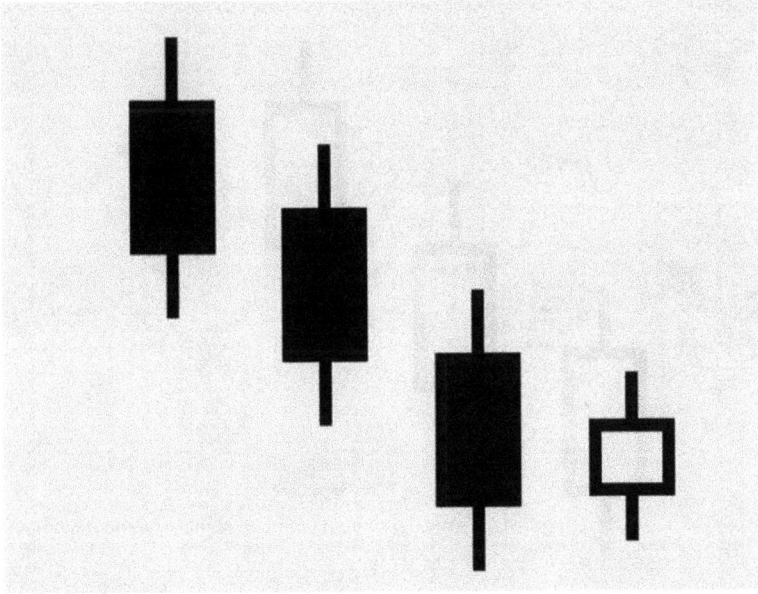

Bearish Harami Cross

A negative harami cross occurs in an uptrend when an up candle is followed by a Doji—a candlestick with virtually identical starting and closing values. The Doji is embedded in the true body of the previous session. A bearish harami has the same ramifications as a bullish harami.

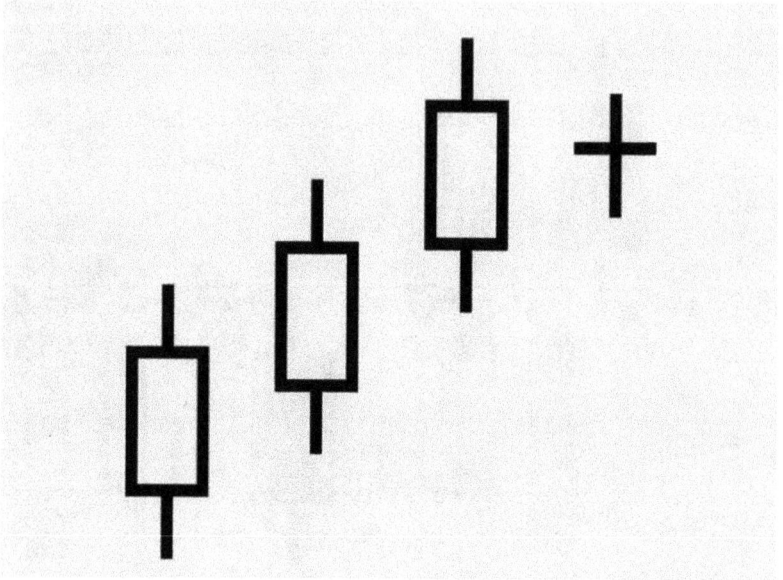

Bullish Harami Cross

A bullish harami cross occurs in a downtrend when a down candle is followed by a Doji. The Doji is embedded in the true body of the previous session. A bullish harami has the same ramifications as a bearish harami.

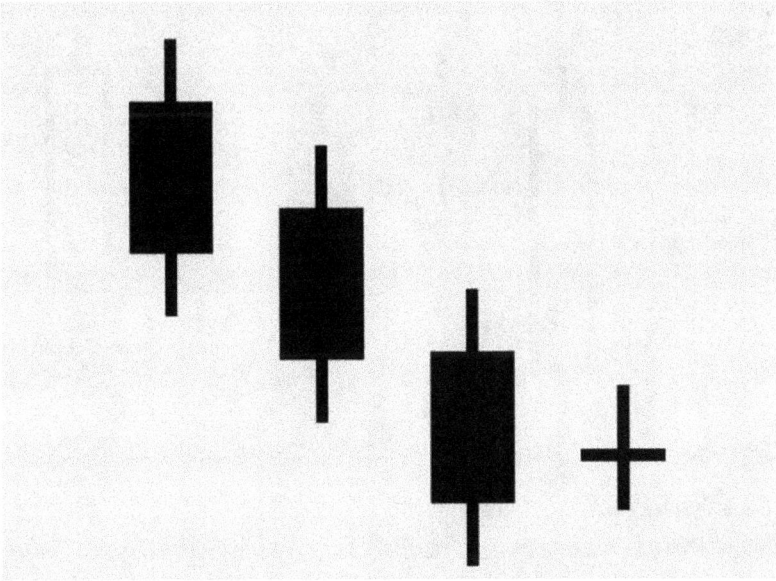

Bullish Rising Three

The pattern starts with a "long white day." Small real bodies then drive the price lower in the second, third, and fourth trading sessions, but they stay within the long Price range on a white day (the first day of the pattern)). The fifth and final day of the pattern is a long white day.

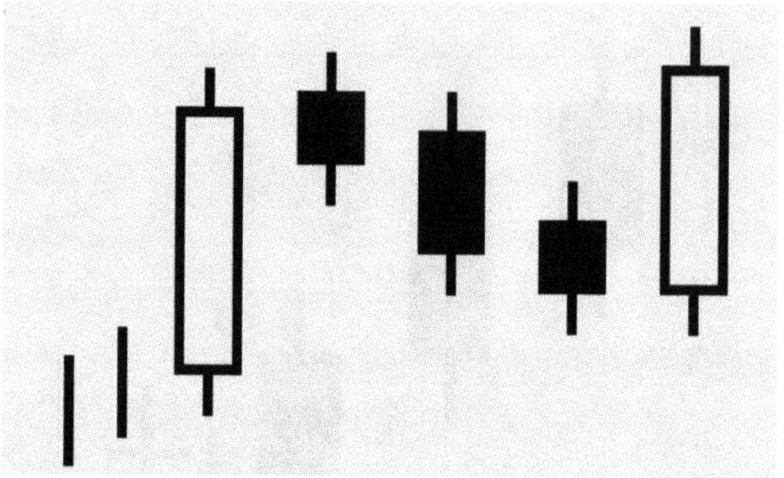

Bearish Falling Three

A major down day kicks off the trend. Three little actual bodies follow climbing but remaining within the range of the first large down day. When the fifth day makes another strong downward swing, the pattern will be complete. It indicates that sellers have recovered market power and that prices may continue to fall.

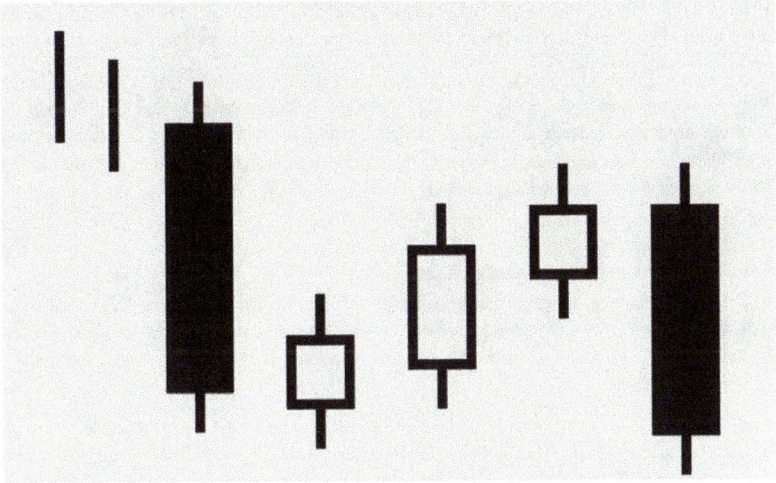

Chapter 3.6: Different Trading Indicators

Traders who trade trends try to recognize and benefit from them. Trend trading is a strategy of earning by determining an asset's momentum in a certain direction; there are several strategies for doing so. In fact, no one technical indication will ensure market success; in addition to technical study, traders must grasp risk management and trading psychology. Certain strategies, on the other hand, have stood the test of time and remain popular among trend traders looking to examine certain market indicators.

Moving Averages

A moving average is a technical analysis approach that smoothes out price data by producing a monthly average price. A moving average provides a single, flat line on a price chart, erasing any deviations caused by random price movements.

The average is calculated over a specified time period, which might be 10 days, 20 minutes, 30 weeks, or any other length specified by the trader. The 200-day, 100-day, and 50-day simple moving averages are popular among investors and long-term trend analyzers.

The moving average may be applied in a number of ways. The first step is to look at the angle of the moving average. If the price moves mostly horizontally over a lengthy period of time, it is not trending; rather, it is ranging. A trading range occurs when a security trades between steady high and low values over an extended period of time.

If the moving average line is tilted upward, an uptrend is underway. Moving averages, on the other hand, do not foretell a stock's future value; rather, they simply represent what the price has done on average over time.

Moving average crossovers are another use. When the 50-day moving average crosses over the 200-day moving average on your chart, you'll get a buy signal. When the 50-day moving average goes below the 200-day moving average, it indicates a sell signal. The time periods can be adjusted to meet your unique trading requirements.

Moving Average Convergence Divergence (MACD)

The MACD (moving average convergence divergence) indicator oscillates. An oscillating indication is a technical analysis indicator that changes over time inside a band (above and below a centerline; the MACD fluctuates above and below zero). It functions as both a trend and a momentum indicator.

One simple MACD strategy is to look at which side of zero the MACD lines are in the histogram beneath the graphic. If the MACD lines are above zero for a lengthy period of time, the stock is expected to rise. If the MACD lines are persistently below zero, the trend is almost likely downward. 2 Possible buy signals emerge when the MACD crosses above zero, and potential sell signals arise when it crosses below zero.

Relative Strength Index (RSI)

The relative power index (RSI) is another oscillating indicator, but its movement range is limited to zero to one hundred, therefore it delivers information distinct from the MACD.

When the histogram indicator is over 70, the price is considered "overbought" and is due for a correction; when the indicator is below 30, the price is considered "oversold" and is due for a bounce.

During a strong upswing, the price will typically remain over 70 for lengthy periods of time. During a downturn, the price may remain at 30 or below for a lengthy period of time. While overall overbought and oversold levels can be correct at times, they may not provide the most timely indications to trend traders.

On-Balance-Volume (OBV)

On-balance volume (OBV) is a relevant indicator in and of itself, and it consolidates a significant quantity of volume data into a single one-line indicator. The indicator adds volume on "up" days and subtracts volume on "down" days to compute cumulative purchasing and selling pressure.

In principle, the volume should confirm trends. If the price rises, the OBV should rise as well; if the price falls, the OBV should decline.

The chart below shows Netflix Inc. 's (NFLX) shares growing with OBV. OBV did not go below its trendline, indicating that the price would likely continue to grow despite the pullbacks.

Chapter 3.7: Creating And Modifying Candlestick

A candlestick chart is a sort of financial chart that shows how the prices of securities change over time.

The following example illustrates how to make a candlestick chart in Excel step by step.

Step 1: Enter the Data

First, input the prices for an 8-day dataset that shows the open, high, low, and closing price for a certain stock:

	A	B	C	D	E	F	G
1	Date	Open	High	Low	Close		
2	1/1/2021	25	28	22	24		
3	1/2/2021	22	27	16	20		
4	1/3/2021	21	29	14	17		
5	1/4/2021	19	25	17	23		
6	1/5/2021	23	24	19	22		
7	1/6/2021	21	26	18	25		
8	1/7/2021	25	31	22	29		
9	1/8/2021	29	37	26	31		
10							
11							
12							
13							
14							
15							
16							
17							
18							
19							
20							
21							
22							

Step 2: Create the Candlestick Chart

Then, as seen below, highlight all of the values in the range A1:E9.

	A	B	C	D	E	F	G
1	Date	Open	High	Low	Close		
2	1/1/2021	25	28	22	24		
3	1/2/2021	22	27	16	20		
4	1/3/2021	21	29	14	17		
5	1/4/2021	19	25	17	23		
6	1/5/2021	23	24	19	22		
7	1/6/2021	21	26	18	25		
8	1/7/2021	25	31	22	29		
9	1/8/2021	29	37	26	31		
10							
11							
12							
13							
14							
15							
16							
17							
18							
19							
20							

Then, along the top ribbon, click the Insert tab. Click the Waterfall symbol in the Charts group, then the Open-High-Low-Close icon:

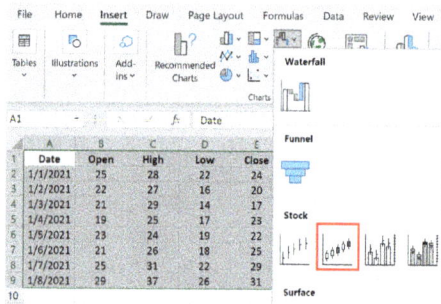

This will generate the candlestick chart shown below:

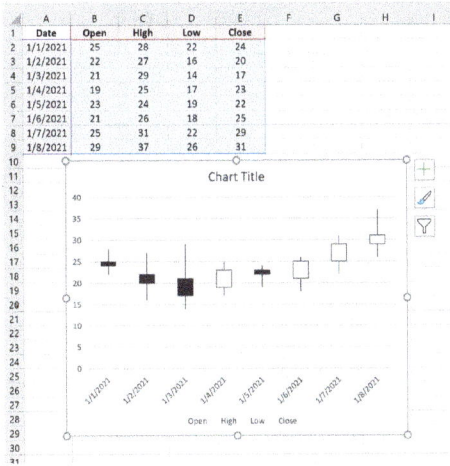

	A	B	C	D	E	F	G	H	I
1	Date	Open	High	Low	Close				
2	1/1/2021	25	28	22	24				
3	1/2/2021	22	27	16	20				
4	1/3/2021	21	29	14	17				
5	1/4/2021	19	25	17	23				
6	1/5/2021	23	24	19	22				
7	1/6/2021	21	26	18	25				
8	1/7/2021	25	31	22	29				
9	1/8/2021	29	37	26	31				

Step 3: Modify the Candlestick Chart

Feel free to give the chart a title and remove the legend at the bottom that states 'Open High Low Close.'

You may also modify the fill colors of the individual candlesticks by clicking on them.

For example, we may alter the color of the 'up' candles to black and the color of the 'down' candles to red:

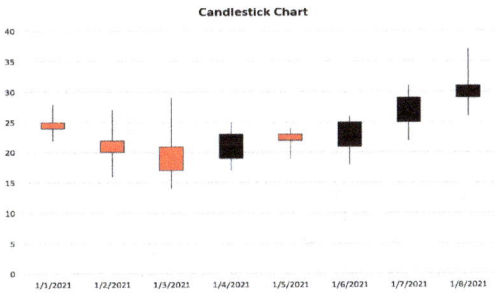

We can now immediately identify which days the stock price finished higher (black) and which days it finished lower (red) (red).

51

Chapter 04: Different Types of Trading

Chapter 4.1: Day Trading
The Basics of Day Trading

Day trading is the act of purchasing and selling securities on a single trading day. It may happen in any market, but the most prevalent are the foreign exchange (FX) and stock markets. The vast majority of day traders are well-educated and financially secure. They use high leverage and short-term trading strategies to capitalize on minor price fluctuations in highly liquid equities or currencies.

Day traders are well aware of the elements that cause short-term market volatility. Trading based on news is a popular approach. Economic statistics, corporate revenues, and interest rates are all influenced by market psychology and expectations. When such expectations are not fulfilled or exceeded, markets respond with rapid, large shifts, which may be quite profitable to day traders.

Day traders employ a variety of intraday methods. These are some of the strategies:

- **Scalping:** Scalping is a trading method that aims to make a series of modest profits based on minor price changes throughout the day.

- **Range Trading:** In range trading, support and resistance levels are commonly employed to make buy and sell decisions.

- **News-based trading:** This approach takes advantage of the increased volatility that occurs in the aftermath of major news events.

- **High-frequency trading (HFT):** Using advanced algorithms, it exploits modest or short-term market inefficiencies.

How day trading works

Volatility is the name of the game in day trading. Day traders rely heavily on stock or market fluctuations to generate money. They prefer companies that fluctuate a lot throughout the day, regardless of the reason: a good or bad earnings report, positive or negative news, or just market mood. They also like highly liquid shares since they may add and exit positions with little influence on the stock's price.

Day traders may buy a stock if it is rising in value or sell it short if it is falling in value, hoping to benefit from the stock's decline. They may trade the same stock multiple times in a day, purchasing one time and then short-selling the next to profit from shifting sentiment. They're searching for a stock to move, no matter which technique they utilize.

Buying on margin

Many traders use borrowed money to perform trades in order to increase profits, a practice known as "buying on margin." Using the assets you already own as leverage, you may borrow up to 50% of the value of the security you want to buy using a margin account. This type of leverage can boost earnings beyond what you could get with your own money, but it also comes with big risks: your losses will be exacerbated.

This is how it goes. You could buy $10,000 worth of stock and borrow the remaining $10,000 from your brokerage business to acquire $20,000 worth of stock. You would have $24,000 if you bought the stock at $10 per share and it rose 20% to $12 per share (and you sold it at that price). After repaying the brokerage business for $10,000, you're left with $14,000, a 40% increase over the $10,000 you put in with your own money. Your return would have been only 20% if you hadn't borrowed money.

But what if the stock price had dropped by 20%? The same rules apply but in reverse. You would only have $16,000 if you sold at $8 per share. You're left with $6,000 after repaying the $10,000 – a 40% loss on your initial investment.

Risks of Day Trading

Due to the multiple risks involved, day trading might be scary for the average investor. The Securities and Exchange Commission (SEC) of the United States has identified some of the hazards associated with day trading, which are summarized below:

- **Expect to lose a lot of money:** Day traders frequently lose a significant amount of money in their first few months of trading, and many never earn a profit, therefore they should only trade with money they can afford to lose.

- **Day trading is a full-time job that is both demanding and expensive:** Day trading is extremely tough, and recognizing market patterns while monitoring hundreds of ticker quotes and price movements requires a high level of concentration. Day traders incur a lot of expenditures since they have to pay their company a lot of money for commissions, training, and computers.

- **Day traders rely heavily on borrowed funds:** Day-trading tactics rely on leverage to earn money, which is why many day traders not only lose all of their money but also end up in debt.

- **Don't be taken in by promises of quick money:** Be wary of "hot ideas" and "professional advice" from day trading newsletters and websites, and keep in mind that educational seminars and workshops on the subject may not be neutral.

Chapter 4.2: Long-Term Trading

A long-term investment strategy is one in which you keep your money for more than a year. Bonds, stocks, exchange-traded funds (ETFs), mutual funds, and other assets are all part of this strategy. Long-term investors must be professional and patient because they must be ready to accept some risk in exchange for higher profits in the long run.

Many market professionals recommend that investors invest in stocks for the long term. Only ten of the 47 years from 1975 to 2021 saw the S& P 500 lose money, making stock market returns very volatile in shorter time frames. Investors, on the other hand, have historically had a far better track record in the long run.

Investors may be tempted to dabble in inequities to enhance short-term profits in a low-interest-rate environment, but it makes more sense—and pays out better overall returns—to keep stocks for the long term. In this post, we'll show you how owning stocks for a longer period of time can pay well.

Long-Term Investments for Companies

On the asset side of a company's balance sheet, a long-term investment represents the company's investments, such as stocks, bonds, real estate, and cash, that it intends to hold for more than a year. When a corporation buys stock or debt from another company as an investment, the classification of the asset as short-term or long-term has an impact on how those assets are valued on the balance sheet.

Short-term investments are marked-to-market, and any value falls are recorded as a loss. Increases in value, on the other hand, are not recognized until the item is sold. This means that determining whether an investment is long- or short-term has a direct impact on the company's reported net income. Analysts watch for changes in long-term assets as a sign that a firm is liquidating assets to fund current expenses, which is usually a bad indicator.

Long-Term Investing for Individuals

Many people's major long-term aim is to save and invest for retirement. While some expenses need a multi-year effort, such as purchasing a car or purchasing and paying off a home, most people have a portfolio for retirement. In this circumstance, we are advised to begin investing early and frequently. Individual investors can leverage the years between now and retirement to take safe risks by combining a long-term vision with the power of compounding. When your time horizon is measured in decades, you can risk market downturns and other hazards in exchange for a larger overall return in the long run.

Common Profile for a Long-Term Investment

Long-term investments are financial instruments that you keep for longer than a year. Most traders hold on to these assets for many years, placing them in portfolios with specific strategies such as 401(k)s, education funds, and long-term savings accounts.

Any asset, just like short-term investments, can be a long-term investment. Long-term investments, on the other hand, continuously improve in value over time, making them ideal assets to hold for many years. Illiquid assets are frequently held by investors as long-term investments.

Real estate is the most prevalent long-term investment. Many individuals buy houses as an investment to keep for years, if not decades, allowing the property's value to rise. The process of buying and selling a house, which makes this investment extremely illiquid, makes it difficult to make a short-term investment, but it is less of an issue over time.

Many mutual funds and bonds are also frequent long-term investments.

Long-term investments, which are portfolios that trade seldom and depend on long-term gains, are used in the majority of retirement accounts and education funds.

Chapter 4.3: Swing Trading
Understanding Swing Trading

Swing trading is a trading method in which investors purchase a stock or other asset and keep it — known as holding a position — for a short length of time (typically a few days to several weeks) in the hopes of profiting.

The swing trader's purpose is to profit from any potential price fluctuation, or "swing," in the market. Individual wins may be less because the trader is focused on short-term trends and tries to eliminate losses as soon as possible. Small profits over time, on the other hand, can add up to a substantial annual return.

How does swing trading work

Swing traders seek trading patterns to purchase or sell stocks in order to profit from market swings and momentum movements. They frequently concentrate on large-cap equities since they are the most actively traded. Because of their high trading volumes, these stocks offer investors insight into how the market perceives the firm and the price fluctuations of its securities. This active trading generates the data needed for technical analysis, which we'll go over in the next section.

Swing traders seek trading patterns to purchase or sell stocks in order to profit from market swings and momentum movements. They frequently concentrate on large-cap equities since they are the most actively traded. Because of their high trading volumes, these stocks offer investors insight into how the market perceives the firm and the price fluctuations of its securities. This active trading generates the data needed for technical analysis, which we'll go over in the next section.

Day Trading vs. Swing Trading

Position holding time is typically the deciding factor between swing trading and day trading. Swing traders often keep their positions overnight, whereas day traders close their positions before the market closes. Day trading positions are kept for a single day, whereas swing trading positions are held for several days to weeks.

Swing traders who hold overnight risk, such as gaps up or down against the position, are subject to the unpredictability of overnight risk. Swing trades are often executed with a lower position size than day trading due to the overnight risk (assuming the two traders have similarly sized accounts). Day traders frequently employ larger position sizes and may require a 25% day trading margin.

Swing traders can also take use of a 50% margin or leverage. This means that if a trader is accepted for margin trading, they just need to put up $25,000 in capital for a $50,000 contract.

Chapter 4.4: Option Trading

Options are contracts that provide the bearer the right, but not the duty, to purchase or sell a certain quantity of an underlying asset at a specified price at or before the contract expires. Options, like most other asset types, may be acquired via brokerage investing accounts.

Options are strong because they can improve a person's portfolio. They do this via increased revenue, protection, and even leverage. There is generally an alternative scenario fit for an investor's purpose depending on the occasion. Using options as an effective hedge against a falling stock market to prevent downside losses is a common example. Options were really designed for hedging reasons. Hedging through options is intended to decrease risk at a low cost. In this case, we may consider choices such as insurance coverage. Options may be used to protect your assets against a downturn in the same way that you would insure your home or vehicle.

How Options Work

It is basically all about evaluating the likelihood of future price occurrences when pricing option contracts. The more probable something is to happen, the more costly a profit-making choice would be. A call option's value increases in tandem with a rise in the underlying stock price. This is crucial in determining the relative worth of choices.

The shorter the period before expiration, the less valuable an option will be. This is because the likelihood of a price movement in the underlying stock decreases as we get closer to expiration. This is why a choice is a squandered asset. If you purchase an out-of-the-money one-month option and the stock does not move, the option loses value with each passing day. Because time is a factor in option pricing, a one-month option will be less valuable than a three-month option. This is because having more time improves the likelihood of a price shift in your favor, and vice versa.

As a result, the identical option strike expiring in a year will cost more than the same strike expiring in one month. Time decay causes this option squandering feature. Even if there is no change in the stock price, the value of an identical option today will be less than it is tomorrow.

How to Trade Options

Many brokers now provide qualifying consumers with access to options trading. If you wish to trade options, you must be authorized by your broker for both margin and options. Once choices have been accepted, there are four fundamental things you may do with them:

1. Buy (long) calls

2. Sell (short) calls

3. Buy (long) puts

4. Sell (short) puts

Purchasing shares results in a long position. Purchasing a call option allows you to take a long position in the underlying stock. Shorting a stock results in a short position. Selling a naked or uncovered call puts you in the position of being short on the underlying stock.

Purchasing a put option allows you to take a short position in the underlying stock. When you sell a naked or unmarried put, you may take a long position in the underlying stock. It is critical to distinguish between these four possibilities.

Option holders are individuals who purchase options, whereas option writers are those who sell options. The key contrast between holders and authors is as follows:

1. Call and put holders (buyers) are not required to purchase or sell. They have the option of using their rights. This restricts the risk of option purchasers to the premium paid.

2. However, call and put writers (sellers) are compelled to purchase or sell if the option expires in the money (more on that below). This implies that a seller may be obligated to fulfill a purchase or sale commitment. It also suggests that option sellers are exposed to additional and in some circumstances limitless, risks. This implies that authors might lose much more than the cost of the option premium.

Options may also provide regular revenue. Furthermore, they are often used for speculative reasons, such as betting on the direction of a stock.

It is important to note that trading fees are normally associated with options trading: a set per-trade cost plus a lesser amount for each contract. For example, $4.95 plus $0.50 per contract.

Chapter 05: Risk Management

Chapter 5.1: Understanding Investing Risk

There will always be some risk in any investment, regardless of the type. To decide whether it's worth putting your money on the line, you must compare the potential benefit against the danger. Understanding the risk-reward relationship is an important part of developing your investment philosophy.

Each investment, such as stocks, bonds, and mutual funds, has its own risk profile, and knowing the distinctions can help you diversify and safeguard your portfolio more efficiently.

To What Extent Are You Willing to Take Risks with Your Investments?

If you maintain your money in traditional savings or money market deposit accounts, you risk falling behind on inflation. However, you run the danger of losing everything if you invest in other sorts of high-reward investments. Only you know how comfortable you are in the following situations:

- **Losing your principal:** You could lose everything if you invest in individual stocks or high-yield bonds.

- **Not keeping pace with inflation:** Your investments may appreciate at a slower rate than the market. If you invest in cash equivalents like Treasury or municipal bonds, this is more likely to happen.

- **Coming up short:** There's a good risk your investments won't provide enough income to meet your retirement requirements.

Paying high fees or other costs: Fees on mutual funds might make it difficult to get a fair return. Be wary of mutual funds that are actively managed or have sales loads.

Chapter 5.2: Common types of Risks in the Stock Market

What causes investment to outperform or underperform unexpectedly? There are several options, starting at the top (the overall picture) and working your way down.

- economic risks,
- industry risks,
- company risks,
- asset class risks,
- market risks.

Risks to the economy as a whole are referred to as economic risks. Inflation or deflation may rise, unemployment may rise, and interest rates may fluctuate as the economic cycle shifts from expansion to recession. These macroeconomic factors have an impact on everyone involved in the economy. The majority of firms are cyclical, meaning they expand when the economy expands and contract when the economy contracts.

When consumers are more confident in economic development and the stability of their employment and salaries, they are more likely to spend more of their discretionary money. They are more ready and able to finance purchases with debit or credit, hence increasing their purchasing power for durable goods. As a result, as an economy grows and businesses grow, demand for most goods and services rises. An

Economic variables that influence an entire industry or technological changes that affect an industry's markets are common examples of industrial hazards. The impact of a rapid spike in the price of oil (a macroeconomic event) on the airline business is a good illustration. An increase in the price of aviation fuel raises airline costs and reduces earnings, and this has an impact on every airline. Interest rate adjustments can have a big impact on a business like real estate. Interest rate hikes, for example, make it more difficult for people to borrow money to fund purchases, lowering real estate values.

The characteristics of specific enterprises or firms that affect their performance and make them more or less vulnerable to economic shocks are referred to as company risk.

An investment's asset class can have an impact on its performance and risk. Investments (assets) are classified according to the markets in which they trade. Asset types are broadly characterized as:

- corporate stock or equity (shares in domestic or foreign public enterprises);
- bonds, or a corporation's or government's public debt;
- Oil, coffee, or gold are examples of commodities or resources.
- depending on the performance of other underlying assets; derivatives or contracts based on the performance of other underlying assets
- real estate (both residential and commercial);

- collectibles and fine art (e.g., stamps, coins, baseball cards, or vintage cars).

There are finer distinctions among those major groups. For example, depending on the size of the firm as defined by its market capitalization, corporate stock is categorized as large-cap, mid-cap, or small-cap (the aggregate value of its stock). Bonds are classified as corporate or government bonds, and their maturity dates determine whether they are short-term, intermediate-term, or long-term.

Risks can have a significant impact on entire asset classes. Changes in the rate of inflation, for example, can make corporate bonds more or less valuable, or less likely to generate desirable yields. Changes in the market can also alter the value of an investment. When the stock market drops sharply and unexpectedly, as it did in October 1929, 1987, and 2008, all equities, regardless of their relative value, are affected.

Categories of Risks

Risk management is classified into two categories: systematic and unsystematic risk, regardless of the specific measures used.

Systematic Risk

Risk management is classified into two groups, systematic and unsystematic risk, in addition to the specific measures.

Unsystematic Risk

Unsystematic risk, the second type of risk, is linked to a company or industry. It's also known as diversifiable risk, and it can be minimized by diversifying your assets. This risk is unique to a certain stock or industry. When an investor buys an oil stock, he is taking on the risk of both the oil sector and the corporation.

Assume an investor owns stock in an oil firm and believes that the price of oil is affecting the company. The investor can take the opposite side of his position, or hedge it, by purchasing a put option on crude oil or the corporation, or he can diversify his risk by purchasing retail or airline shares.

Chapter 5.3: The Greeks

Understanding the Geeks

The Greeks are the factors that are used to estimate risk in the options market. Each of these dangers is denoted by a Greek symbol.

Each Greek variable is the outcome of a flaw in the option's assumption or link to another underlying variable. Traders use Greek values such as delta, theta, and others to evaluate options risk and manage option portfolios.

Greeks encompass a wide range of characteristics. Delta, theta, gamma, vega, and rho are only a few of them. Each of these Greeks has a numerical value that informs traders about how the option moves or the risk connected with it. Each of the major Greeks (delta, vega, theta, gamma, and rho) is calculated as a percentage.

Some Important Greeks to Understand
Delta

The rate of change between the option's price and a $1 change in the underlying asset's price is represented by the delta (). In other words, the option's price sensitivity is proportional to the underlying asset. A call option's delta can be anywhere between 0 and 1, while a put option's delta can be anywhere between 0 and -1. Consider the case of a holder of a long 0.50 delta call option. As a result, if the underlying stock's price climbs by $1, the option's price rises by 50 cents.

Delta is also the hedging ratio used by options traders to build a delta-neutral position. For example, if you buy a conventional American call option with a delta of 0.40, you'll have to pay

Theta

Theta () denotes the rate of change in the option price as a function of time, also known as time sensitivity or time decay. All other conditions being equal, theta reflects how much an option's price lowers as the time to expiry decreases. Let's look at the situation of a long (or bullish) -0.50 theta option investor. If all other factors remained constant, the price of the option would decrease by 50 cents each day.

When options are in the money, theta rises; when options are out of the money, theta falls. Options with a shorter time to expiry decay quicker. Theta is favorable for short calls and puts and negative for long calls and puts. In contrast, an item whose worth does not deteriorate over time, such as a

Gamma

The rate of change between the delta of an option and the price of the underlying asset is represented by gamma (). It's known as second-order (second-derivative) price sensitivity. The gamma number is the amount by which the delta would change if the underlying securities moved $1. Consider the case of an investor who is long a call option on the fictitious stock

XYZ. The call option has a delta of 0.50 and a gamma of 0.10. As a result, if stock XYZ increases or decreases by $1, the delta of the call option increases or decreases by 0.10.

Options traders may choose to hedge not only delta but also gamma to achieve delta-gamma neutrality, which means that the delta will remain close to zero while the underlying price fluctuates.

Vega

The rate of change between the value of an option and the implied volatility of the underlying asset is represented by Vega (v). This measures how much the option is affected by changes in volatility. The Vega indicator shows how much an option's price changes in response to a 1% change in implied volatility. A vega of 0.10, for example, indicates that the option's value is likely to move by 10 cents if the implied volatility changes by 1%.

Increased volatility implies that the underlying instrument is more likely to experience extreme values, hence a rise in volatility raises the option's value. A decrease in volatility, on the other hand, will have a negative impact on the option's value. For at-the-money options with extended expiry durations, Vega is at its peak.

The gamma coefficient is used to determine how stable the delta of an option is: Higher gamma values imply that the delta could alter drastically in response to even minor price changes in the underlying. As expiry approaches, gamma increases in magnitude for at-the-money options and decreases for in- and out-of-the-money options. As the expiry date approaches, the gamma value drops; options with longer expirations are less susceptible to delta changes. Since expiration approaches, gamma readings often rise as price swings have a bigger impact on gamma.

Rho

The rate of change between the value of an option and a 1% change in the interest rate is represented by Rho (). This is an interest rate sensitivity metric. Assume that a call option with a rho of 0.05 and a price of $1.25 has the same rho and price as a put option with the same rho and price. The call option's value rises to $1.30 if interest rates rise by 1%, provided all other conditions remain unchanged. Put options, on the other hand, are the antithesis of call options. Rho works best with options that are at the money and have a long expiry term.

Minor Greeks

Lambda, epsilon, vomma, vera, zomma, and ultima are some additional Greeks that aren't as well-known. These Greeks are pricing model derivatives that impact, among other things, delta changes in reaction to volatility variations. These complicated and even esoteric risk concerns are becoming more common in options trading techniques because computer software can swiftly calculate and adjust for them.

Chapter 5.4: Common Methods of Measurement for Investment Risk

Investment decisions can't be made without considering and addressing the risks involved. The technique comprises identifying and analyzing the level of risk associated with an investment before accepting or mitigating it. Some common risk metrics include standard deviation, beta, value at risk (VaR), and conditional value at risk (CVaR).

1. Standard Deviation

The standard deviation quantifies how far data deviates from its anticipated value. The standard deviation is used to measure the degree of historical volatility associated with a certain investment in proportion to its yearly rate of return when making an investment choice. It depicts how far the current return deviates from historical typical returns. For example, a stock with a high standard deviation has a higher level of volatility and, as a result, a higher level of risk.

The semi-deviation effectively merely looks at the standard deviations to the downside for individuals who are only interested in potential losses and ignore potential gains.

2. Sharpe Ratio

The Sharpe ratio is a risk-adjusted performance metric. This is done by deducting the rate of return on a risk-free investment, such as a U.S. Treasury bill. Treasury Bonds, based on the rate of return.

This is then divided by the standard deviation of the related investment to determine whether the return is attributable to prudent investing or the assumption of excessive risk.

The Sortino ratio, which excludes the impacts of upward price movements on standard deviation to focus on the distribution of returns that are below the goal or necessary return, is a version of the Sharpe ratio. In the numerator of the formula, the Sortino ratio replaces the risk-free rate with the needed return, resulting in the Sortino ratio.

3. Beta

Another typical risk metric is beta. Beta is a metric that measures the degree of systematic risk that an individual security or industry sector has in contrast to the broader stock market. One is the market's beta, which can be used to gauge the risk of a security. When a security's beta is equal to one, its price moves in lockstep with the market. A beta greater than one indicates that an investment is more volatile than the market as a whole.

A beta of less than one, on the other hand, indicates that a security is less volatile than the market. Let's say a security's beta version is 1.5. In theory, the security is 50% more volatile than the market.

4. Value at Risk (VaR)

Value at Risk (VaR) is a statistical measure used to quantify the level of risk associated with a portfolio or organization. The VaR calculates the highest likely loss with a degree of confidence for a particular period. Consider a $5 million investment portfolio with a one-year 10% VaR. As a result, the portfolio has a 10% probability of losing more than $5 million over the course of a year.

5. Conditional Value at Risk (CVaR)

Another risk indicator used to analyze an investment's tail risk is the conditional value at risk (CVaR). The CVaR, which is used as an extension to the VaR, assesses the likelihood of a break in the VaR with a certain degree of confidence; it seeks to estimate the probability of a break in the VaR with a particular degree of confidence. This statistic is more sensitive to events that happen at the tail end of a distribution, sometimes called tail risk. Assume a risk manager believes that the average investment loss for the worst one percent of conceivable portfolio outcomes is $10 million. As a result, the CVaR, or estimated shortfall, for the 1% tail is $10 million.

6. R-squared

R-squared is the percentage of a fund portfolio or safety's movements that can be described by movements in a benchmark index. The benchmark for fixed-income securities and bond funds is the US Treasury Bill. The S&P 500 Index serves as a benchmark for stocks and mutual funds.

The range of R-squared values is 0 to 100. A mutual fund with an R-squared rating of 85 to 100 has a performance record that is closely associated with the index, according to Morningstar. A fund rated 70 or below is unlikely to outperform the index.

Investors in mutual funds should avoid actively managed funds with high R-squared ratios, which are sometimes referred to as "closet" index funds by analysts. For this reason, it is often wise to

Chapter 5.5: Introduction to Standard Deviation

Understanding the Standard Deviation

The standard deviation is a statistic that measures the dispersion of a dataset about its mean by calculating the square root of the variance. The standard deviation is calculated as the square root of variance by computing each data point's difference from the mean.

When data points are further from the mean, there is more variance within the data set; as a result, the larger the standard deviation, the more spread out the data is.

Standard deviation is a financial statistical measure that exposes an investment's historical volatility when applied to its annual rate of return.

The bigger the difference between each price and the mean, the greater the standard deviation of securities.

The Formula for Standard Deviation

$$\text{Standard Deviation} = \sqrt{\frac{\sum_{i=1}^{n} (x_i - \bar{x})^2}{n - 1}}$$

where:

x_i = Value of the ith point in the data set

$\bar{x}$ = The mean value of the data set

n = The number of data points in the data set

Calculating the Standard Deviation

Standard deviation is calculated as follows:

1. The mean value is derived by multiplying the total number of data points by the number of data points.

2. Each data point's variance is computed by subtracting the mean from the data point's value. After that, each of the resulting numbers is squared, and the sum is calculated. The output is then divided by one divided by the total number of data points.

3. The standard deviation is calculated using the square root of the variance (result from no. 2).

Chapter 5.6: Different Risk Management Strategies

Risk is a constant in our lives. Taking risks or avoiding taking chances, all rely on the decisions we make. However, the greatest risk that one can incur is not taking chances.

In the stock market, the link between risk and return is strong. Correct risk management strategy reduces losses and provides traders with information about future market developments. For instance, a trader who has made significant gains might lose them all in a single transaction if no risk management plan is in place.

Planning your Trades

A trading strategy allows traders to effortlessly trade in the markets since the criteria are pre-set.

Planning trades helps you understand when to take gains and reduce losses, which may help you remove emotions from the decision-making process.

With a strategy in hand, comes the discipline to stick to it. You could learn why certain trades work and others don't.

It also allows you to learn from prior trading blunders and improve your decision-making skills for future trades.

A trading strategy must include the following parameters:

- Motivation for trading
- Time commitment
- Trading Goals
- Attitude towards Risk
- Availability of Capital
- Markets you want to trade
- Steps for record-keeping

The One-Percent Rule

The "1 percent risk rule" is one of the most successful risk management measures. Adherence to this criterion limits capital losses when a trader encounters tough and intolerable market circumstances. This regulation restricts the risk on any particular deal to no more than 1% of the entire account value of the trader.

Traders may risk 1% of their money by trading huge positions with tight stop-losses or tiny positions with stop-losses positioned far away from the entry price.

It is impossible to win every deal, and the 1% risk rule helps to keep a trader's money from plummeting dramatically in adverse and inevitable circumstances.

This rule may be used for trading in the stock market as well as other markets such as futures or FX. This strategy enables you to profit regardless of market circumstances, whether tumultuous or calm.

Calculating Expected Returns

The degree of risk connected with trading in the markets is usually proportional to the level of return that a trader might expect.

The goal of estimating anticipated return is to provide an investor an indication of likely reward against risk.

An anticipated return is computed by multiplying hypothetical outcomes by the probability that they will occur and then adding the results.

It is a method used to evaluate if the average net result of a deal is positive or negative. It is often based on previous data and hence cannot be guaranteed for the future; yet, it frequently establishes acceptable predictions.

Effectively Set Stop-Loss And Take Profit Points

Stop-loss orders protect traders from losing too much money in a single deal. Taking profits, on the other hand, allows traders to lock in their gains.

It is important since the market is unpredictable. At one time, things are going well, and at another, the market is bearish. The elements supporting bearish markets may be evaluated fundamentally or technically, but the trader may have already suffered all of the losses.

Diversification and Hedging

Diversification aids in optimizing profits by investing in several sectors that might respond differently in comparable situations. Although it does not guarantee protection against losses, diversity is the most crucial component of achieving long-term investment objectives while potentially decreasing unanticipated risks.

Hedging assists traders and investors in reducing risk and volatility by lowering the potential of loss. The inclusion of uncorrelated equities in a portfolio reduces overall volatility. Simply put, traders hedge one investment by placing a transaction in another in order to balance the market's risk and reward parameters.

Chapter 06: Trading Strategies

Chapter 6.1: Trading Strategies - Basics

An analysis-based plan used to pinpoint specific market circumstances and price levels is known as a trading strategy. Although fundamental analysis can be used to forecast price changes, the majority of tactics concentrate on particular technical indications.

What distinguishes a trading strategy from a trading style?

Although the terms "style" and "strategy" are frequently used interchangeably, there are several critical distinctions that every trader should be aware of. A trading strategy is a very particular process for determining at which price points you will join and exit deals, as opposed to a trading style, which is an overall plan for how frequently you will trade and how long you will hold positions open for.

Your preferences when trading a market or asset, such as how regularly and for how long or short a time frame, are known as your trading style. The market's behavior can cause a trader's style to alter, but whether you decide to adjust or wait till the market is more favorable will depend on your goals.

Best trading strategies

We've examined a few of the most well-liked top-level trading tactics, such as:

1. Trend trading

2. Range trading

3. Breakout trading

4. Reversal trading

5. Gap trading

6. Pairs trading

7. Arbitrage

8. Momentum trading

Chapter 6.2: Trend trading

A trend trading technique depends on determining the direction of market momentum through technical analysis. Since each position will stay open as long as the trend persists, this is typically seen as a medium-term technique that works best with swing trading or position trading.

An asset's price may trend upward or downward. When you think the market would hit higher highs is when you would take a long position, if you were going to do so. If you believed that the market would make lower lows, you would take a short position.

Because they allow traders to go long and short, derivative and leveraged products, like CFDs, are popular candidates for trend-following techniques. In this case, you would start a larger position by making a small initial deposit (known as a margin). Because your overall profit or loss is reliant on the size of all your positions, leveraged trading carries significant risk, and you run the danger of losing more than your initial deposit. Ensure that you have effective risk management procedures in place.

Throughout the trend, trend traders will utilize indicators to spot probable retracements, which are transient movements against the main trend. Retracements are frequently ignored by trend traders, but it's crucial to make sure they don't signify a complete turnaround, which would be a hint to exit the trade.

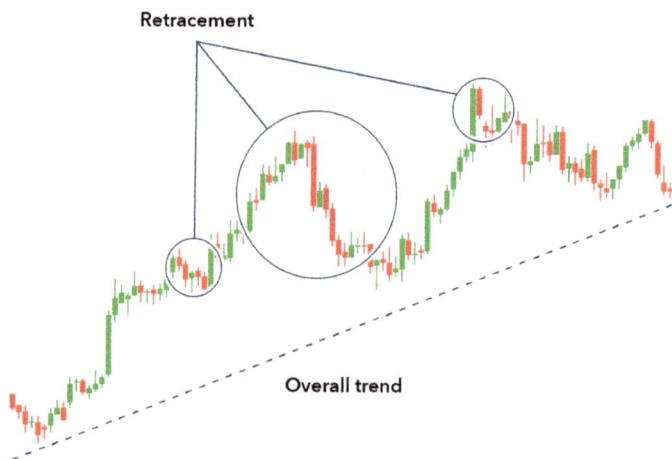

Retracement

Overall trend

Moving averages, the relative strength index (RSI), and the average directional index are some of the most widely used technical analysis tools used in trend-following techniques (ADX).

Chapter 6.3: Range trading

The goal of range trading is to make money in stable market conditions. If the price of an asset consistently hovers between two levels of technical support and resistance, analysts say the market is consolidating. Range trading is common across timeframes and trading styles, although it is most common among day traders and other short-term traders (sometimes known as scalpers) due to the strategy's emphasis on taking short-term gains.

Those who trade in the range will focus on smaller price swings, while those who trade with the trend will look at the bigger picture. They will enter long bets when the price is trading between two predetermined levels without touching either one.

Since many forex traders think the extremely liquid currency market maintains a small trading range with high volatility between these levels, this strategy has become popular. Traders with a shorter time horizon may attempt to benefit from the price action around key support and resistance levels.

The stochastic oscillator and the relative strength index (RSI) are two more indicators that range traders may use to identify overbought and oversold conditions. Range traders also utilize technical analysis tools like the Bollinger band and fractals to assess if and when the market price will break out of the range they have established.

Chapter 6.4: Breakout trading

The goal of breakout trading is to enter a trend as early as possible, waiting for the price to "break out" of a range. Day traders and swing traders frequently employ breakout trading because it takes advantage of short- to medium-term market changes.

By entering the market at the right level, these breakout traders may ride the movement from beginning to end. Traders that employ this approach look for price points that signify the beginning of a period of volatility or a change in market mood. Around levels of support or resistance, limit-entry orders are frequently placed, ensuring that any breakout instantly executes a transaction.

The majority of breakout trading methods are based on volume levels since the premise holds that as volume levels begin to rise, a breakout from a support or resistance level will soon occur. As a result, common indicators include the volume-weighted moving average, on-balance volume, and the money flow index (MFI).

Breakout

Resistance
level

Support
level

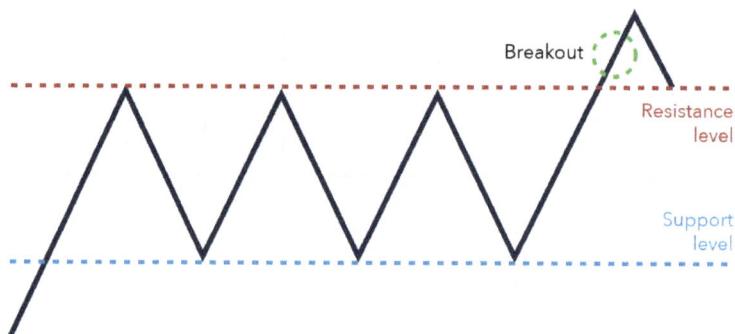

Chapter 6.5: Reversal trading

Predicting when a trend will change direction is the basis of the reversal trading approach. Once the reversal has occurred, the technique will resemble a trend trading strategy a lot because it can endure for a variety of lengths of time.

Since this is only a change in how the market feels, the trend might reverse in any way. The market is near the bottom of a downtrend and is about to transition into an uptrend, according to a "bullish reversal." A "bearish reversal" on the other hand signifies that the market is at the peak of an upswing and is most likely to move downward.

It's crucial to confirm that the market is not merely retracing when trading reversals. A frequently utilized tool to determine whether the market has beyond recognized retracement levels is the Fibonacci retracement. It's important to note that some people believe that Fibonacci retracements are self-fulfilling prophecies since numerous orders will gather around them and drive the market in the desired direction.

Chapter 6.6: Other Types of Trading Strategies

It is crucial to use technical indicators in conjunction with other analytical techniques, including fundamental analysis and other technical instruments.

Gap trading

Where there has been no trading activity, a gap forms. This occurs when the price of an asset jumps abruptly high or low with no time in between, indicating that the market began at a different price than when it last closed.

If you trade gaps, you probably trade during the day and look for opportunities between these gaps and the trading range that begins the following day. An opportunity to go long is typically represented by an opening range that is higher than the close of the previous day, while an opening range that is lower than the close of the previous day typically represents an opportunity to go short.

Pairs trading

Pairs trading involves buying underpriced products and selling overpriced ones by identifying associated pairs of instruments where the valuation connection has changed. Regardless of market conditions, such as downtrends or uptrends, the goal is to turn a profit.

Arbitrage

A trade or series of transactions that involve arbitrage allows you to make money without taking any risks. Identifying a chance between two equivalent assets where one is priced more than the other and taking advantage of purchasing the lower-priced asset while it is still undervalued would be an illustration of this. Few arbitrage possibilities exist because numerous traders may also be searching for them, and they are frequently discovered fast. In this instance, the arbitrage advantage quickly vanishes as other traders swarm the market in an effort to take advantage of the chance.

Momentum

Price movements and the path they are following are the foundation of the momentum trading method. This occurs when traders are buying and selling assets for an extended period of time and there is significant price movement (or momentum). The momentum shifts in a different direction after a price adjustment.

Chapter 6.7: Finding the Best Strategy for you

When it comes to trading, there is no one approach that fits all, and no two people will have the same precise plan. Your level of motivation, your trading style, your appetite for risk, and other factors will all affect which approach will perform best for you.

Before entering the live markets, always conduct as much research as you can. If you want to hone your abilities, sign up for a trial account.

What to know before implementing your trading strategy

Implementing your plan may need patience, commitment, and practice. You can start with a sample account and test your strategy there without taking any risks. Even more, when you sign up, you'll receive CHF 20,000 in virtual money to practice with.

Additionally, you can use the demo account to learn about the markets and develop your regular trading routine. You'll have access to a variety of platforms once you're prepared to compete in the live markets. Our cutting-edge web platform, our acclaimed mobile app, or specialist platforms like MT4, L2 Dealer, and Realtime are all options. Free trade alerts are another perk you can use to obtain notifications that are automatic and can be customized when your trading parameters are met. Additionally, trading signals that offer effective buy-and-sell advice

Chapter 07: Being a Successful Investor

Chapter 7.1: Finding the Sources of Stock Performance Predictions
Methods of Stock Market Prediction

1. Fundamental Analysis

2. Technical Analysis

Here are more specifics on these approaches that assist investors in doing the research before making an investment choice on a certain company.

Fundamental Analysis

Fundamental analysis is the process of determining the worth of a stock by researching aspects that may influence its price. It might be due to either internal or external forces. Internal considerations might include the company's financial health, future prospects, the market in which it works, the management, the prospects of the industry in which it operates, and broader global and national economic circumstances.

There are two methods basic analysis is commonly done.

- Top-Down Approach
- Bottom-Up Approach

Commonly used metrics in Fundamental analysis are

Some of the ratios utilized in the basic analysis are listed below.

- **Earnings per share**

- **Price to Earnings ratio**

- **Return on equity**

One of the most crucial indicators of a company's success is its return on equity. A greater ROI assures investors of the company's profitability, which will ultimately lead to a rise in trading volume and stock prices.

- **Price to Earnings to growth ratio**

- **Price to book ratio**

Technical Analysis

Technical analysis is a method of measuring a company's performance using certain technical characteristics. Technical analysis is the study of a stock's current day performance in order to forecast its movement the next day based on specific characteristics. Expert analysts are more likely to employ this form of analysis than typical investors. Technical indications or pointers assist an investor in better assessing the stock and making investment choices that optimize their profits.

Common technical analysis metrics

- Simple Moving averages
- Exponential moving averages
- Candlestick patterns
- Volume breakouts
- Momentum indicators

Chapter 7.2: How to Become a Successful Stock Market Investor

To begin with, investors are people who have a long-term perspective on stock markets. They choose a good stock and stick with it until the complete tale develops and presents itself. So, is there something like Successful Investment Strategies or a Bible that instructs us on How to Become a Successful Share Market Investor? To be honest neither exists! You have guidelines and some pearls of knowledge to help you become a successful investor. As previously said, effective investing entails three critical steps: discovering a Good Story, sticking with the Good Stories for an extended period of time, and departing losers soon. Only by mastering these three processes will you be able to become a successful investor. The following are the 7 Habits of Highly Successful Investors.

1. Make a legally enforceable pledge to your long-term investing plan.

A long-term plan is one of the most important things you can do to be a successful investor. Themes that hold you in the long term are key to successful investing plans. As an investor, your primary aim is to mix the best of growth and value. Growth firms will provide a virtuous cycle of positive price movement, P/E re-rating, and profit growth to match these valuation re-ratings. A sound investing plan is built on two essential elements. To begin, you take a value strategy and aim to invest in future leaders at cheap values. Eicher in 2009 and Escorts in 2012 were both instances of companies trading at steep discounts. When the firm begins to perform well, the values rise, and you should consider it a growth stock. The most essential thing is to stick to this investing strategy.

2. Diversify your risk; there is no great merit in concentration.

There is a small contradiction here. Successful investors may tell you that they made the majority of their money in only a few stocks. That is completely correct! However, in order to live long enough in the markets to generate money, you must carefully control your risk. Here is where variety comes into play. Too much concentration may kill your stock account, therefore you must continually evaluate your risk. Whether you are a trader or an investor, one of your primary aims is to protect cash, which can only be accomplished by diversifying your risk.

3. Never overtrade the market and always keep an eye on expenses.

These are two distinct challenges with significant significance. Your route to being a successful investor starts with cost management. Costs have a wide range of impacts. There are transaction costs, regulatory costs, lost opportunity costs, and taxes expenses to consider. The key to successful investing ideas is to limit your expenditures to a bare minimum. It makes a significant impact on your portfolio over time.

4. Before putting down any money on a stock, be sure you know all there is to know about it.

The ability to recognize attractive stocks is one of the seven characteristics of extremely successful investors. It is not just about buying a stock, but also about timing your purchase. If you had invested in any of the downturns during the previous ten years, your returns would have been far higher. Before investing, learn about the firm, its business strategy, its key competitors, and potential disruptions. Determine if the company has a moat and a margin of safety, and concentrate on intangible assets. Successful investing techniques are all about picking the appropriate stock and joining at the correct moment. Concentrate on doing your best and don't stress about capturing the bottom and top of any stock.

5. You should cut your losses as quickly as feasible.

The key to being a good stock market investor is to eliminate your lost investments. A wise investor would never average holdings in the hope that the stock will recover. It all comes down to conviction. Even the smartest investors can only get 70% of their predictions accurate. You must guarantee that the remaining 30% of your portfolio's duds do not consume your resources and time needlessly, resulting in opportunity losses.

6. Make your money last as long as possible.

This is the difference between winners and ultra-winners among the seven behaviors of very successful investors. If you purchased Eicher in 2009 for Rs.200 and sold it three years later for Rs.1000, you would have earned a lot of money. But you would have missed out on the enormous admiration that you would have received if you had stayed. Concentrate on your conviction rather than the percentage returns you have earned. In 1980, an Rs.10,000 investment in Wipro grew to about Rs.300 crore by 1999. As a result, how to become a great investor in the stock market is all about unwavering confidence and the patience to let gains run as long as feasible.

7. As an investor your focus should be on risk-premiums.

Buying into risk premiums is key to successful investing strategies. You cannot become a successful investor unless you are willing to take risks. Great transactions in history, such as Tudor Jones purchasing on Black Friday in 1987 or John Paulson shorting subprime in 2006-07, were all about risk premiums. As an investor, you have many possibilities to earn good money and only a few opportunities to make a lot of money. These large possibilities will truly establish you as a great investor, and it all comes down to concentrating on the risk premium. That implies the rewards are almost certainly vastly more than the risk you are incurring.

Chapter 7.3: Traits of Every Successful Investor to Follow

A competent investor uses his money and invests the remainder; an ordinary investor uses his money and invests the rest. A successful investor weighs potential risks against potential returns. While some have gained millions, many others have lost. To become a competent investor, learn the essential traits of one.

Goal setting

A smart investor will always have a specific aim in mind. It is critical to have a strategy in place to attain your objectives. Variations are most likely to draw an investor's attention away from the agenda. A skilled investor will have a plan of action in place within a certain time frame for a specific return on investment. They are prepared for market instability, and their strategies are generally developed with both sides in mind.

Knowledge

A competent investor, in addition to making the greatest use of time, is knowledgeable about the market. He or she knows the fund's position and has done a study on the company's investing strategy and philosophy. You should be aware of how your money is being used. A competent investor examines the company's development trend over time using reliable sources. A smart investor will also have a clear exit point based on their expectations and expertise. A good investor is an active learner who is willing to make the proper decision based on actual information.

Right Decision

A wise investor understands the passage of time. They are aware of the current market scenario. They keep up to date on market activity and growth. Having a solid awareness of trends allows investors to see beyond their objectives and determine the length of the investment. A competent investor understands current developments and the company's market position. They accept responsibility for their errors and learn not to repeat them. A competent investor does not have to follow trends; he or she just does what is right.

Patience

Because of his patience, a successful investor builds money over time. It is most likely the best characteristic to have. A good investor believes in his ideas. They normally do not feel guilty about the 10% decrease; instead, they choose to wait for the 100% increase. They are adamant about adhering to their ideas. They seldom participate in the purchase and sell trends.

Risk Aversion

A good investor understands the inherent risk in investing. They comprehend their strategies and assess their potential rewards. Being risk averse is a trait molded by experience, knowledge, and trust in the important attributes listed above.

Chapter 7.4: Tips for Succeeding in Your Investing Career

While the stock market is fraught with volatility, some tried-and-true rules may help investors improve their long-term prospects of success.

Some investors lock in gains by selling valued equities while retaining underperforming stocks in the belief that they would recover. However, excellent stocks might continue to rise, while bad ones face extinction.

Ride a Winner

Peter Lynch famously mentioned "tenbaggers," or assets that soared in value tenfold. His success was ascribed to a modest handful of these companies in his portfolio.

However, if he believed there was still tremendous upside potential, he needed the discipline to hold onto equities even after they had climbed by several multiples.

The key point is to avoid sticking to artificial standards and instead evaluate a stock on its own merits.

Sell a Loser

There is no assurance that a stock will recover after a prolonged slump, and it is critical to be realistic about the possibility of underperforming investments. And, although admitting to losing stocks might psychologically imply failure, there is no shame in admitting errors and selling off assets to avoid additional loss.

Don't Sweat the Small Stuff

Rather than being concerned with an investment's short-term swings, it is best to monitor its long-term direction. Have faith in the long-term narrative of an investment and don't be persuaded by short-term volatility.

Don't overestimate the few pennies you could save by utilizing a limit order instead of a market order. Yes, active traders profit from minute-to-minute changes. Long-term investors, on the other hand, succeed over time spans of years or more.

Don't Chase a Hot Tip

Never believe a stock tip, regardless of its source. Before investing your money, always do your own research on a firm.

Tips do sometimes work, depending on the legitimacy of the source, but long-term success requires extensive investigation.

Pick a Strategy and Stick With It

There are several techniques for stock picking, and it is necessary to follow a certain philosophy. Changing your strategy basically turns you into a market timer, which is risky ground.

Consider how famed investor Warren Buffett kept to his value-oriented approach and avoided the late-'90s dotcom boom, averting big losses when tech businesses imploded.

Don't Overemphasize the P/E Ratio

Investors place a lot of weight on price-earnings ratios, but it's hazardous to focus too much on a single signal. When paired with other analytical processes, P/E ratios perform best.

As a result, a low P/E ratio does not always indicate that a security is cheap, nor does a high P/E ratio indicate that a firm is overpriced.

Maintain a Long-Term Perspective and Concentrate on the Future

Investing necessitates making educated judgments based on future events. Past data may predict the future, but it is never certain.

Chapter 7.5: Controlling Your Emotions With The Stock Market And Not Letting Your Emotions Win

To maximize profits in the stock market, years of skill and a deep grasp of market dynamics are required. Trading, as opposed to investing, includes the frequent purchasing and selling of assets.

Among the many things you should avoid while trading is trading with your emotions. Emotional trading has various drawbacks and may lead to considerable monetary loss. Here are several reasons why emotions should not influence your trading.

Emotional Effects of Stock Market Trading

Exposes You to Unnecessary Risk

Stock market trading is a dangerous endeavor in and of itself, with several systematic and unsystematic hazards to consider. While there are several techniques for mitigating these risks, trading on emotions leads to a myopic approach, which increases the quantum of risk exponentially. Whatever stock you are trading, you must comprehend its fundamentals as well as the company's corporate governance strategy.

To increase your wealth, it is recommended to trade (buy and sell) stocks with strong fundamentals. However, while trading emotionally, you often overlook these critical facts. For example, when markets are undergoing an amazing bull run, there is a worry of losing out on performing rounds. Many investors believe that if they do not invest now, they will miss the bus.

They tend to neglect important parts of trading in the process and may wind up betting on companies with bad fundamentals. This considerably increases the magnitude of risk, and there is a considerable danger of capital loss. As a result, it is important to keep your emotions under control and proceed with the activity.

This results in trading that is not in line with your objectives.

It is critical to link your trading and investing strategies with your objectives. Goal-based investing ensures that funds are there when you need them. When you trade emotionally, though, you tend to accept calls that do not do credit to this idea. To put it another way, it keeps you distant from the big picture and causes you to focus on the short term. This might have a negative impact on wealth generation.

When you trade unemotionally, your decisions are based on logic, facts, and data. You trade in accordance with your objectives and make accurate decisions. This not only increases your money but also provides a pleasurable experience.

At the same time, it assists you in better navigating the market, understanding the influence of numerous market forces, and developing a sound plan to enhance your earnings.

Makes Your Trading Experience Pleasant

Another reason is to ensure that there is no place for emotion in trading. Stock markets are an excellent location to build money, providing you are willing to remain dedicated and avoid taking shortcuts to success. Shortcuts often result in poor selections that might ruin the whole experience. It's no different with emotions.

Whether you trade out of fear or greed, you run the risk of having a bad experience. A poor encounter, particularly during formative trading days, might be depressing and put you off markets for good. Many investors have abandoned markets after a bad experience, depriving themselves of the potential to maximize their capital.

Stock markets, especially stocks, have the ability to outperform inflation. They also assist you to diversify your portfolio by providing a variety of different financial products. However, if a bad experience causes you to abandon markets entirely, the loss is ultimately yours.

Makes You Indulge in Revenge Trading

You are more inclined to participate in revenge trading if you lose money due to emotional trading. This trading refers to the practice of continuing with a transaction in order to recover from a prior loss. There is a strong desire to recover from the loss as soon as possible, and in order to do so, you engage in random deals that may do more damage than good.

The threat does not stop there. Revenge trading may also lead to overtrading, which can drastically increase your expenditures. Stress levels rise, and there is a greater likelihood of making too many wrong decisions. When you trade unemotionally, though, things might be quite different.

If things aren't going your way, you may call it a day, figure out what went wrong, and take remedial actions to assure success the next time you trade.

Ways to Control Emotions

Formulate Your Plan

Every trader is unique. To keep your emotions in control, develop a trading plan based on your requirements and market expertise. Set your risk thresholds and benchmarks for when to enter and depart. Continue to revise the strategy to verify you are on the correct road.

Block Market Noises

Market sounds might cause emotional outbursts. There will be a lot of noise whether markets are in a bull or bear period. Not all sounds are insignificant, but permitting them all might have an influence on your trading approach and decisions. To keep your emotions under control, you must filter out the noise.

Think Logically

Logical reasoning may assist you in keeping your emotions under control. When you think rationally, you make sensible judgments that help you earn money. Always ask yourself if your choice is emotionally motivated or based on facts.

Chapter 7.6: Dreaming the Bigger Picture

Many new traders struggle to accept a cold, hard reality about trading: you can't become wealthy overnight. You must just take it one day at a time and achieve a relatively tiny profit throughout a number of deals. This is something that experienced traders are aware of. They may expect to earn large gains in the long term, but on any given day, they are just concerned with generating as many respectable profits as possible, rather than a single, life-changing deal.

Many traders are aware of this truth, yet it is difficult to accept. Many people are driven to trade in the anticipation of generating large gains that may be utilized to fund a wealthy, exciting lifestyle. Or money that may be utilized to demonstrate to family and friends that one is worthy of jealousy or admiration. However, approaching trading from this angle is risky. It immediately opposes the notion that it would take some time to earn enough money to sustain a new lifestyle or impress others.

What's the danger in wishing for great fortune? Nothing if you know it's all a dream. If you don't, you may want to take action. If you fantasize about how massive wins may improve your life, you'll begin to want extraordinarily large earnings, and you'll likely begin to take steps to get these big wins even when low-risk possibilities are unavailable. You may engage in larger, riskier deals with the intention of tripling your wealth. Alternatively, you may be tempted to deviate from your trading strategy because you perceive the possibility of a large profit. You may even forsake all risk controls if you begin to believe, "Unless I can earn a lot of money quickly, trading isn't worth it anyhow."

It's critical to maintain your modesty. It is improbable that you will be financially secure for the rest of your life following only a few large deals. You will have to work long and hard hours, just like other seasoned and successful traders. It is critical for your survival that you maintain the appropriate viewpoint. Someday you could be rich and live an exciting lifestyle, but it won't happen tomorrow or even in the next year. Don't worry about tomorrow just yet; focus on now. Concentrate on the process of learning to trade. Trading is enjoyable, and you should take advantage of it.

When you adopt this viewpoint, you will be pleased with your trading results regardless of how well you perform. And you will trade more calmly and objectively if you follow a comprehensive trading strategy, apply adequate risk management, and just strive for a decent, realistic profit. You'll begin to amass riches, and maybe, in time, you'll amass enough money to realize your wildest goals. But, for the time being, the only things that can help you become a consistently successful trader are hard effort, reasonable objectives, and tenacity.